Enrichment Workbook

STRETCH YOUR THINKING

TEACHER'S EDITION
Grade 4

Harcourt Brace & Company

Orlando • Atlanta • Austin • Boston • San Francisco • Chicago • Dallas • New York • Toronto • London

http://www.hbschool.com

Copyright © by Harcourt Brace & Company

All rights reserved. No part of this publication may be reproduced or
transmitted in any form or by any means, electronic or mechanical,
including photocopy, recording, or any information storage and retrieval
system, without permission in writing from the publisher.

Requests for permission to make copies of any part of the work should
be mailed to: Permissions Department, Harcourt Brace & Company,
6277 Sea Harbor Drive, Orlando, Florida 32887-6777.

HARCOURT BRACE and Quill Design is a registered trademark of
Harcourt Brace & Company. MATH ADVANTAGE is a trademark of
Harcourt Brace & Company.

Printed in the United States of America

ISBN 0-15-311090-2

5 6 7 8 9 10 085 2000

CONTENTS

Par for the Course

In golf the **par** for a hole is the number of strokes, or hits, it takes an average golfer to put the ball in the hole.

If a golfer is **under par**, it means that he or she took less than the par number of strokes to put the ball in the hole.

If a golfer is **over par**, it means that he or she took more than the par number of strokes to put the ball in the hole.

par for the hole: 4
golfer's strokes: 1 under par
golfer's score: $4 - 1 = 3$

par for the hole: 4
golfer's strokes: 2 over par
golfer's score: $4 + 2 = 6$

Find the golfer's score for each hole.

1.

Par: 3
Strokes: 1 under par

Score: __2__

2.

Par: 4
Strokes: 1 under par

Score: __3__

3.

Par: 3
Strokes: 1 over par

Score: __4__

4.
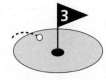

Par: 2
Strokes: par

Score: __2__

5.

Par: 3
Strokes: 2 over par

Score: __5__

6.

Par: 5
Strokes: 2 under par

Score: __3__

7. **a.** Add the par numbers for the holes to find the par for the course.

Par for the course: __20__

b. Add the golfer's scores for the holes to find her or his score for the course.

Score for the course: __19__

c. Was the golfer over or under par for the course? By how much?

__under par; 1 stroke__

Harcourt Brace School Publishers

STRETCH YOUR THINKING   E1

Name _____

Balance It

Write the expressions from the box below above the pans of the scales so that the two amounts on a scale are the same.

8 + 9	7 + 7	3 + 8	20 − 6
5 + 6	12 − 4	15 + 0	9 − 1
11 + 6	18 − 3	9 + 9	14 − 2
11 + 7	6 + 6	17 − 8	13 − 4

Possible answers are shown.

1.   __7__ + __7__   __20__ − __6__

2.   __8__ + __9__   __11__ + __6__

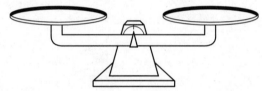
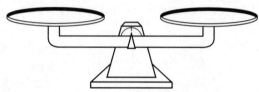

3.   __12__ − __4__   __9__ − __1__

4.   __15__ + __0__   __18__ − __3__

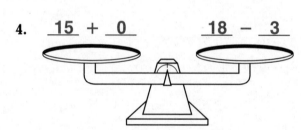

5.   __3__ + __8__   __5__ + __6__

6.   __6__ + __6__   __14__ − __2__

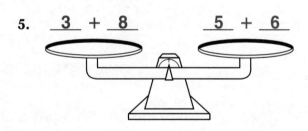
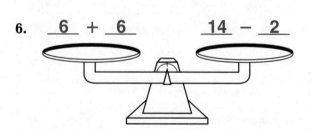

7.   __13__ − __4__   __17__ − __8__

8.   __9__ + __9__   __11__ + __7__

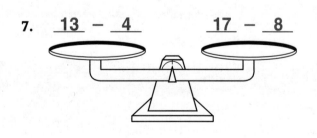
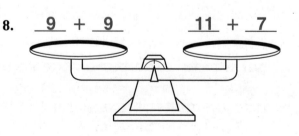

Harcourt Brace School Publishers

E2   STRETCH YOUR THINKING

Calendar Calculations

Month:	Calendars will vary, depending on month.					

Look at a classroom calendar and copy this month's dates.

1. Look at the 3 × 3 box outlined on the calendar. Add the three numbers along each diagonal in this box. A diagonal is from corner to corner as shown by the dashed lines on the calendar. **Addition sentences will vary, but sums should be the same.**

____ + ____ + ____ = ____ and ____ + ____ + ____ = ____

2. Outline another 3 × 3 box on the calendar. Add the three numbers along each diagonal in the box. **Addition sentences will vary, but sums should be the same.**

____ + ____ + ____ = ____ and ____ + ____ + ____ = ____

3. What do you notice about the sums of the numbers along the diagonal in a 3 × 3 box on the calendar?

The sums are the same.

4. What do you think you will find if you add the numbers along the diagonal of a 4 × 4 box on the calendar? **Answers will vary.**

Try it to see. **Addition sentences will vary, but sums should be the same.**

____ + ____ + ____ + ____ = ____

____ + ____ + ____ + ____ = ____

Harcourt Brace School Publishers

Design a Zoo

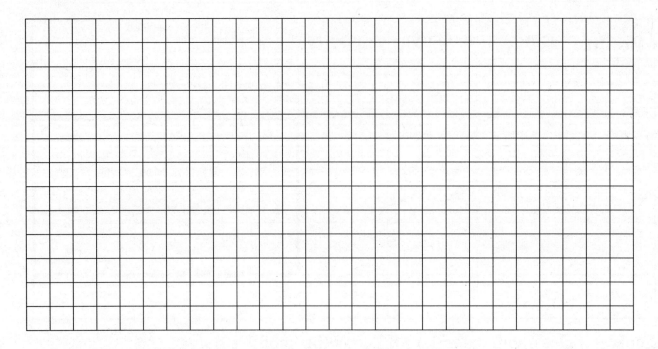

Design your own zoo.
- Choose eight animals.
- Outline on the grid above some space for each animal.
- Label each space with a letter from *A* to *H*.
- Record the perimeter of each animal space.
  Animals and perimeters will vary.

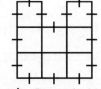

Sample: Penguin House
perimeter = 14 units

1. Animal A
animal

_____

perimeter

_____

2. Animal B
animal

_____

perimeter

_____

3. Animal C
animal

_____

perimeter

_____

4. Animal D
animal

_____

perimeter

_____

5. Animal E
animal

_____

perimeter

_____

6. Animal F
animal

_____

perimeter

_____

7. Animal G
animal

_____

perimeter

_____

8. Animal H
animal

_____

perimeter

_____

Harcourt Brace School Publishers

How Long?

Estimate the length or height of each animal.
Choose the closest measure from the box.
Write the measure and the letter next to it.

a. 8 ft	l. 18 in.	b. 6 ft
u. 4 ft	w. 5 ft	e. 30 in.
h. 9 ft	e. 6 in.	l. 11 ft

1.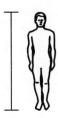

height ___6 ft___

letter ___b___

2.

height ___11 ft___

letter ___l___

3.

length ___4 ft___

letter ___u___

4.

length ___6 in.___

letter ___e___

5.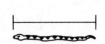

length ___5 ft___

letter ___w___

6.

height ___9 ft___

letter ___h___

7.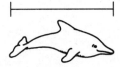

length ___8 ft___

letter ___a___

8.

height ___18 in.___

letter ___l___

9.

height ___30 in.___

letter ___e___

10. Write the letters from Exercises 1–9 in order to complete
this sentence.

A _b_ _l_ _u_ _e_ _w_ _h_ _a_ _l_ _e_ can grow
to 100 feet long!

Harcourt Brace School Publishers

Money Math

Write each amount from the box below in a money bag to make
the number sentences true.

$6.45	$21.07	$13.10	$23.06
$16.32	$4.48	$10.99	$8.93

1. $16.85 − **$8.93** = $7.92

2. **$13.10** + $5.76 = $18.86

3. $6.90 + $4.09 = **$10.99**

4. $22.57 − **$6.45** = $16.12

5. $9.23 + $11.84 = **$21.07**

6. **$23.06** − $4.56 = $18.50

7. $19.45 − **$4.48** = $14.97

8. **$16.32** + $11.63 = $27.95

9. If you put the money from each money bag into one large
money bag, will you be putting in an amount that is
greater than or less than $100?

greater than $100

Harcourt Brace School Publishers

Roman Numerals

The ancient Romans used letters as numerals.

I	V	X	L	C	D	M
1	5	10	50	100	500	1,000

If the letter for a lesser value comes before that of a greater value, the lesser value is subtracted from the greater value. Otherwise, the values are added. To find the value:

XII = 10 + 2, or 12

IV = 5 − 1, or 4

Step 1—Circle any instances of a lesser value coming before a greater value.

Subtract those values.

Step 2—Add together all the values.

Example 1	Example 2
LXIX	CVII
↓	↓
LX ⓘX	CVII
↓	↓
10 − 1 = 9	↓
↓	↓
50 + 10 + 9 = 69	100 + 5 + 1 + 1 = 107

Write the number. Find the number in the code box.
Write the corresponding letter in the answer box.

93	374	29	1415	57	770	1900	550
o	e	s	o	s	l	u	m

1. LVII

_57_ | s |

2. XXIX

_29_ | s |

3. XCIII

_93_ | o |

4. DL

_550_ | m |

5. MCM

_1900_ | u |

6. MCDXV

_1415_ | o |

7. CCCLXXIV

_374_ | e |

8. DCCLXX

_770_ | l |

Write each letter on the line above its exercise number to find the answer to this question:

9. What was the arena called where the Romans held sporting events?

The _c_ _o_ _l_ _o_ _s_ _s_ _e_ _u_ _m_
    3.   8.   6.   2.   1.   7.   5.   4.

Harcourt Brace School Publishers

STRETCH YOUR THINKING E7

Four Hundred to None

Take turns with a partner. You each play the game on your own page. You need a 0–9 spinner and base-ten blocks.

1. Start with 4 hundreds blocks.

2. Spin twice. Use the two numbers to write a 2-digit number in the white space after the minus sign.

3. Subtract that value from your base-ten blocks. Regroup your blocks when you need to.

4. Record the number of hundreds, tens, and ones blocks you have left in the next white space below 400.

5. The player who reaches zero first, or has the least value of base-ten blocks when the page is finished, wins.

Game results will vary.

H	T	O	Start
4	0	0	
			—
			—
			—
			—

H	T	O	
			—
			—
			—
			—

Finish

Harcourt Brace School Publishers

Going Up!

Use the code to write the elevation, in feet, of each of these United States mountains.

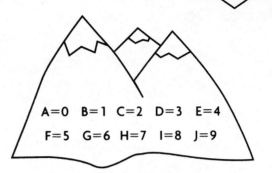

A=0 B=1 C=2 D=3 E=4

F=5 G=6 H=7 I=8 J=9

1. Humphreys Peak, Arizona
BCGDD

___12,633 ft___

2. Mt. Enotah, Georgia
EHIE

___4,784 ft___

3. Harney Peak, South Dakota
HCEC

___7,242 ft___

4. Castle Peak, Idaho
BBICA

___11,820 ft___

5. Mt. Washington, New Hampshire
GCII

___6,288 ft___

6. Mt. Whitney, California
BEEJE

___14,494 ft___

7. Mt. McKinley, Alaska
CADCA

___20,320 ft___

8. Mt. Marcy, New York
FDEE

___5,344 ft___

9. Mt. Elbert, Colorado
BEEDD

___14,433 ft___

10. Which mountain is the highest? the lowest?

___**Mt. McKinley; Mt. Enotah**___

Use the information on mountain elevations to write a word problem. **Problems will vary.**

11. _____

_____

_____

_____

_____

Harcourt Brace School Publishers

Miles to Go

Mileage Chart	Charleston, SC	Jacksonville, FL	New Orleans, LA	New York, NY	Raleigh, NC	Tallahassee, FL	Washington, DC
Charleston, SC		239	781	764	281	404	525
Jacksonville, FL	239		546	940	455	165	702
New Orleans, LA	781	546		1,324	860	390	1,085
New York, NY	764	940	1,324		492	1,105	238
Raleigh, NC	281	455	860	492		615	256
Tallahassee, FL	404	165	390	1,105	615		868
Washington, DC	525	702	1,085	238	256	868	

Follow these steps to find the driving distance between
New York City, NY, and Tallahassee, FL.

• Locate New York City along the top of the chart.
  Locate Tallahassee along the side of the chart.

• Follow the column down, and the row across.

• The number at which they intersect is the driving
  distance, in miles, between them.

So, the driving distance between New York City and
Tallahassee is 1,105 miles.

The Coronado family traveled from New York City to Charleston,
SC, in 3 days. Use the mileage chart to find the number of miles
they traveled each day.

1.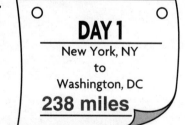

DAY 1
New York, NY
to
Washington, DC
238 miles

2.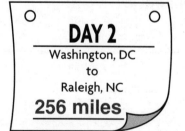

DAY 2
Washington, DC
to
Raleigh, NC
256 miles

3.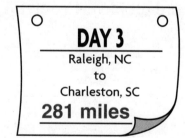

DAY 3
Raleigh, NC
to
Charleston, SC
281 miles

4. On which day did they travel the greatest distance?
   the least distance?

Day 3; Day 1

Harcourt Brace School Publishers

Dog-Gone It!

Erica dropped the information cards she had arranged for her report on dogs. She needs to match each breed of dog with its weight card.

170 lb   52 lb   66 lb

18 lb   27 lb   63 lb

Read the clues below. Then write each dog's weight on the card below it.

Clues:

- The golden retriever weighs about 70 pounds.

- The St. Bernard weighs the most.

- The Scottish terrier weighs about 50 pounds less than the golden retriever.

- The greyhound and the golden retriever together weigh about 130 pounds.

- The beagle weighs more than the Scottish terrier, but less than the basset hound.

1.

Greyhound
63 lb

2.

Scottish Terrier
18 lb

3.

Basset Hound
52 lb

4.

Golden Retriever
66 lb

5.

St. Bernard
170 lb

6.

Beagle
27 lb

Harcourt Brace School Publishers

Plus or Minus

When there is more than one addition or subtraction sign in
a sentence, add or subtract from left to right.

$13 + 5 - 9 = ?$

$13 + 5 = 18$

$18 - 9 = 9$

So, $13 + 5 - 9 = 9$.

$20 - 10 - 7 = ?$

$20 - 10 = 10$

$10 - 7 = 3$

So, $20 - 10 - 7 = 3$.

$15 - 8 + 4 = ?$

$15 - 8 = 7$

$7 + 4 = 11$

So, $15 - 8 + 4 = 11$.

Write + or − in each ◯ to complete the sentence. Use a
calculator to check your work.

1. 7 $\ominus$ 2 $\oplus$ 10 = 15

2. 16 $\ominus$ 3 $\ominus$ 5 = 8

3. 12 $\oplus$ 4 $\ominus$ 9 = 7

4. 2 $\oplus$ 8 $\oplus$ 6 = 16

5. 14 $\oplus$ 3 $\ominus$ 5 = 12

6. 25 $\ominus$ 9 $\oplus$ 1 = 17

7. 30 $\oplus$ 10 $\oplus$ 5 = 45

8. 80 $\ominus$ 40 $\ominus$ 20 = 20

Write six sentences of your own. **Sentences will vary.**

9. _____ ◯ _____ ◯ _____ = _____

10. _____ ◯ _____ ◯ _____ = _____

11. _____ ◯ _____ ◯ _____ = _____

12. _____ ◯ _____ ◯ _____ = _____

13. _____ ◯ _____ ◯ _____ = _____

14. _____ ◯ _____ ◯ _____ = _____

Harcourt Brace School Publishers

E12   STRETCH YOUR THINKING

Clamshells, Pebbles, and Sticks

The Mayan number system used only 3 symbols.

0	●	———
0	1	5

Here are some Mayan numbers:

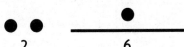

| 2 | 6 | 10 | 13 |

Complete the information card. Use Mayan numbers. **Answers will vary. All numbers should be Mayan numbers.**

Information About _____

Age _____ Date of Birth _____

Telephone Number ____ ____ ____ – ____ ____ ____ ____

Address : _____

_____

Number of brothers and sisters _____

Number of pets _____

I learned to _____ when I was _____ years old.

Harcourt Brace School Publishers

Chartered Territory

Property of One	Zero Property	Order Property
$3 \times 1 = 3$	$6 \times 0 = 0$	$2 \times 5 = 10$ $5 \times 2 = 10$

1. Use the multiplication properties to complete the multiplication chart.

×	0	1	2	3	4	5	6	7	8	9
0	0	0	0	0	0	0	0	0	0	0
1	0	1	2	3	4	5	6	7	8	9
2	0	2	4	6	8	10	12	14	16	18
3	0	3	6	9	12	15	18	21	24	27
4	0	4	8	12	16	20	24	28	32	36
5	0	5	10	15	20	25	30	35	40	45
6	0	6	12	18	24	30	36	42	48	54
7	0	7	14	21	28	35	42	49	56	63
8	0	8	16	24	32	40	48	56	64	72
9	0	9	18	27	36	45	54	63	72	81

2. Look for patterns in the multiplication chart. Explain one pattern that you see. **Possible answer: If you read along diagonal lines, there are interesting patterns. For example, from 3 to 3, the numbers are 0, 2, 2, 0; from 4 to 4, the numbers are 0, 3, 4, 3, 0.**

3. Suppose you added two more rows to the bottom of the chart. What would the numbers in each row be?

10, 0, 10, 20, 30, 40, 50, 60, 70, 80, 90;

11, 0, 11, 22, 33, 44, 55, 66, 77, 88, 99

Harcourt Brace School Publishers

Fingers and Factors

Mickey's mother taught him how to multiply by using his fingers. She said this is a very old method. It only works when the factors are greater than 5. Here are the steps Mickey followed to find the product of 7 × 8.

Step 1 7 is 2 more than 5. Turn down 2 fingers of the left hand.

Step 2 8 is 3 more than 5. Turn down 3 fingers of the right hand.

Step 3 Multiply the number of turned-down fingers by 10.

$5 \times 10 = 50$

Step 4 Multiply the number of *not* turned-down fingers of one hand by the number of *not* turned-down fingers of the other hand.

$3 \times 2 = 6$

Step 5 Add the products.
So, 7 × 8 = 56

$50 + 6 = 56$

Use the above method to find the product.

1. 6 × 8 = __48__

2. 6 × 6 = __36__

3. 7 × 7 = __49__

4. 7 × 9 = __63__

5. 9 × 8 = __72__

6. 6 × 7 = __42__

7. 9 × 9 = __81__

8. 6 × 9 = __54__

9. 8 × 8 = __64__

10. 7 × 6 = __42__

11. 8 × 7 = __56__

12. 9 × 6 = __54__

13. 8 × 6 = __48__

14. 9 × 7 = __63__

15. 8 × 9 = __72__

Harcourt Brace School Publishers

Up, Down, or Diagonal

Find three numbers in a row that have the given product. Draw a line through the three numbers. You may draw the line across, up and down, or diagonally.

1. product: 36

1	2	5
6	3	0
7	6	2

2. product: 120

2	9	5
3	5	7
5	6	4

3. product: 90

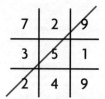

7	2	9
3	5	1
2	4	9

4. product: 60

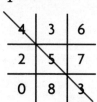

4	3	6
2	5	7
0	8	3

5. product: 96

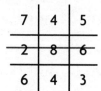

7	4	5
2	8	6
6	4	3

6. product: 126

2	8	6
6	3	4
9	7	2

7. product: 96

5	3	4
4	2	8
7	9	3

8. product: 135

5	6	2
9	7	4
3	2	8

9. product: 210

7	6	5
1	4	7
9	5	3

10. product: 144

9	7	3
2	8	6
7	4	2

11. product: 168

4	5	3
8	0	7
6	9	8

12. product: 64

6	5	3
4	4	4
7	8	9

13. Make your own puzzle. Exchange with a partner to solve.

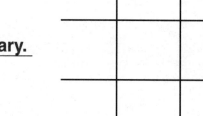

product: **Answers will vary.**

Harcourt Brace School Publishers

Quilt Design

Design a colorful pattern that follows the rules. You will need crayons.

Rules

1. Color the squares to make areas of red, green, or blue rectangles or squares.

2. Color the following numbers of squares.

    54 squares must be red
    36 squares must be green
    24 squares must be blue
    30 squares must be white **Possible design is shown.**

R	R	R	G	G	G	G	G	G	R	R	R
R	R	R	G	G	G	G	G	G	R	R	R
R	R	R					B	B	R	R	R
		B	B	B		B	B				
		B	B	B		B	B	R	R	R	
R	R	R	G	G	G	G	G	G	R	R	R
R	R	R	G	G	G	G	G	G	R	R	R
R	R	R	B	B		B	B	B			
		B	B		B	B	B				
R	R	R	B	B				R	R	R	
R	R	R	G	G	G	G	G	G	R	R	R
R	R	R	G	G	G	G	G	G	R	R	R

Harcourt Brace School Publishers

Birthday Greetings

Grandma Gallagher will soon be 75 years old. Her ten
grandchildren made a card to give her on her birthday.
They will sign their names in order from oldest to youngest.

**Use the clues below to find the age of each grandchild. Record the
names in the chart.**

1. Ryan is 8 years old.

2. Nadia is 5 years younger than Ryan.

3. Nick is 6 times as old as Nadia.

4. Mary Kate is 4 years older than Ryan.

5. Emma is 2 years older than Nadia.

6. Charlotte is half as old as Mary Kate.

7. Jack is 4 times as old as Emma.

8. Margaret is 4 years older than Charlotte.

9. Laura is 7 years younger than Nick.

10. Michael is twice as old as Ryan.

For Problems 11–12, use the chart.

11. Who will sign the card first? last?

   ____Jack; Nadia____

12. Who will be the fifth person to

   sign the card? _____Laura_____

20 yr	Jack
19 yr	
18 yr	Nick
17 yr	
16 yr	Michael
15 yr	
14 yr	
13 yr	
12 yr	Mary Kate
11 yr	Laura
10 yr	Margaret
9 yr	
8 yr	Ryan
7 yr	
6 yr	Charlotte
5 yr	Emma
4 yr	
3 yr	Nadia

Harcourt Brace School Publishers

Word Wise

1. Circle each word in the puzzle below. The words may be written across, down, upside down, or diagonally.

sum	quotient	product	difference	dividend
factor	minus	divisor	remainder	addend

E	F	A	D	I	S	U	M	U	W	I	N
C	Y	M	U	T	U	B	I	H	C	T	H
N	O	I	F	A	C	T	O	R	A	N	P
E	U	N	J	D	T	N	E	D	R	E	O
R	Q	U	P	F	F	D	K	I	S	I	M
E	C	S	U	G	N	L	E	V	H	T	P
F	B	O	N	I	D	I	V	I	S	O	R
F	X	S	A	D	D	E	N	D	Q	U	E
I	J	M	K	E	U	W	H	E	Y	Q	X
D	E	R	V	L	M	A	I	N	D	R	S
R	E	T	O	A	P	R	O	D	U	C	T

2. Write each puzzle word under the operation sign with which it belongs.

+	−	×	÷
sum	minus	factor	divisor
addend	difference	product	dividend
			quotient
			remainder

Mad Math

Play with a partner. Follow these steps:

- Player 1 thinks of a division fact.

- Player 2 tries to identify the fact by guessing the digits in it.

- For each correct guess Player 1 writes the digit in each place it appears in the fact. For each incorrect guess Player 1 draws a feature in one of the four sections of the face—either an eye or a mouth.

- Play continues until either Player 2 guesses the fact or Player 1 completes the face.

- Players switch roles.

1.

___ ___ ÷ ___ = ___

2.
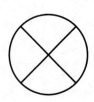

___ ___ ÷ ___ = ___

3.

___ ___ ÷ ___ = ___

4.
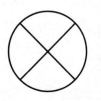

___ ___ ÷ ___ = ___

5.

___ ___ ÷ ___ = ___

6.
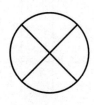

___ ___ ÷ ___ = ___

7.

___ ___ ÷ ___ = ___

8.

___ ___ ÷ ___ = ___

9.

___ ___ ÷ ___ = ___

10.

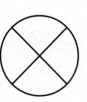

___ ___ ÷ ___ = ___

11.

___ ___ ÷ ___ = ___

12.
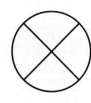

___ ___ ÷ ___ = ___

Harcourt Brace School Publishers

Remainder Roll

Play with a partner. Take turns. You will need a number cube.

- Roll the number cube.

- Choose a number from the box. Cross out the number. Divide it by the number you rolled.

- Record the remainder as your score. If there is no remainder, record a zero.

- Add to find your total score. The player with the lower score at the end of 8 rounds is the winner.

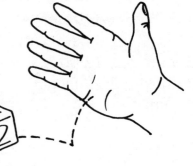

14	33	26	6	29	11	32	10
21	9	18	15	30	24	19	23

Answers will vary.

Player 1

_____

+ _____

+ _____

+ _____

+ _____

+ _____

+ _____

+ _____

My total score: _____

Player 2

_____

+ _____

+ _____

+ _____

+ _____

+ _____

+ _____

+ _____

My total score: _____

Harcourt Brace School Publishers

Time Travel

The world is divided into time zones. If you travel from one time zone to another, you need to set your watch forward or backward to match the time in the new time zone.

The clocks below show you what time it is in several cities in the United States when it is 1:00 P.M. in Boston, Massachusetts. Remember, 12:00 A.M. is midnight, 12:00 P.M. is noon.

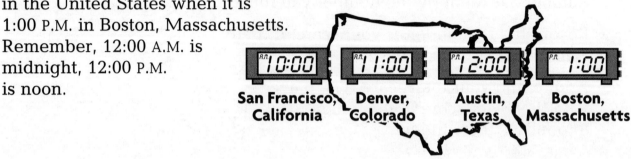

San Francisco, California **Denver, Colorado** **Austin, Texas** **Boston, Massachusetts**

Complete the table.

	San Francisco, CA	Denver, CO	Austin, TX	Boston, MA
1.	10:00 A.M.	11:00 A.M.	12:00 P.M.	1:00 P.M.
2.	11:00 A.M.	12:00 P.M.	1:00 P.M.	2:00 P.M.
3.	12:00 P.M.	1:00 P.M.	2:00 P.M.	3:00 P.M.
4.	10:00 P.M.	11:00 P.M.	12:00 A.M.	1:00 A.M.
5.	11:00 P.M.	12:00 A.M.	1:00 A.M.	2:00 A.M.

Use the information in the table to solve the problem.

6. Debbie lives in Denver. She is going to call her aunt who lives in Boston. At what time should Debbie make her call if she wants to reach her aunt when it is 6:00 P.M. in Boston?

_____ 4:00 P.M. _____

7. Jeremy's favorite football team is playing in Austin. The game starts at 3:00 P.M. At what time should Jeremy turn on his television in San Francisco if he wants to watch the game?

_____ 1:00 P.M. _____

Write a problem using the information in the table.
Exchange papers with a partner. Solve.

8. _____ **Problems will vary.** _____

Harcourt Brace School Publishers

Division Dilemma

Play with a partner. You will need a paper clip and a calculator.

- Take turns.

- Use the paper clip and your pencil on the spinner. Spin for a divisor.

- On the gameboard cross out all the numbers that can be divided by that divisor and have no remainder.

- Your partner should check your work. Use a calculator if it is helpful.

- The player who crosses out the last number is the winner.

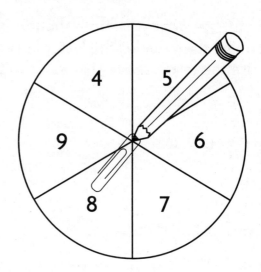

45	14	32	72	21
30	54	24	16	36
42	18	40	25	63
28	64	15	56	48
49	27	81	35	20

Harcourt Brace School Publishers

Letter Logic

Riddle: Why can't a nose be 12 inches long?

To find out, use what you know about multiplication and division to determine the value of the letter in each number sentence. Then write the letter above that value in the answer box below.

1. $9 \div t = 9$ $t = \underline{\quad 1 \quad}$

2. $8 \times 6 = 6 \times w$ $w = \underline{\quad 8 \quad}$

3. $5 \times 0 = u$ $u = \underline{\quad 0 \quad}$

4. $1 \times a = 3$ $a = \underline{\quad 3 \quad}$

5. $6 \div n = 1$ $n = \underline{\quad 6 \quad}$

6. $(2 \times 7) \times 3 = e \times (7 \times 3)$ $e = \underline{\quad 2 \quad}$

7. $h \div 7 = 1$ $h = \underline{\quad 7 \quad}$

8. $3 \times 12 = l \times 3$ $l = \underline{\quad 12 \quad}$

9. $i \times 1 = 5$ $i = \underline{\quad 5 \quad}$

10. $13 \div 1 = c$ $c = \underline{\quad 13 \quad}$

11. $6 \times (10 \times 2) = (6 \times d) \times 2$ $d = \underline{\quad 10 \quad}$

12. $7 \times s = 4 \times 7$ $s = \underline{\quad 4 \quad}$

13. $b \div 1 = 9$ $b = \underline{\quad 9 \quad}$

14. $f \times 3 = 3 \times 14$ $f = \underline{\quad 14 \quad}$

Answer Box

B	E	C	A	U	S	E		T	H	E	N		I	T
9	2	13	3	0	4	2		1	7	2	6		5	1

W	O		U	L	D		B	E		A		F	O	O	T	!
8			0	12	10		9	2		3		14			1	

Harcourt Brace School Publishers

Math Machinery

Each machine in Mariko's Machinery Shop does different things
with the numbers put into it.

Complete the *In* and *Out* panels on each machine.

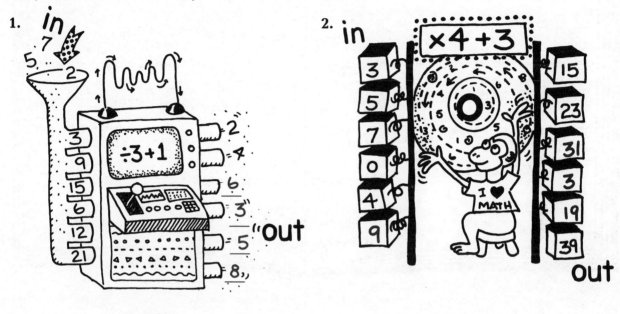

1. *in* 7 5 2

÷3+1

3
9
15
6
12
21

2
7
6
3
5
8
out

2. *in* ×4+3

3
5
7
0
4
9

15
23
31
3
19
39

I ♥ MATH

out

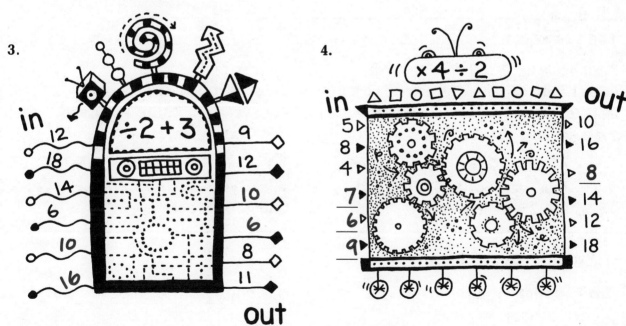

3. *in* ÷2+3

12
18
14
6
10
16

9
12
10
6
8
11

out

4. ×4÷2

in *out*

5 → 10
8 → 16
4 → 8
7 → 14
6 → 12
9 → 18

5. The machine in Problem 4 needs to be reprogrammed to
do the same job in one step instead of two. How can this
be done?

   Have the machine multiply the number put into it by 2.

Harcourt Brace School Publishers

Calendar Conundrums

1. Use a calendar to fill in the missing words of the rhyme.

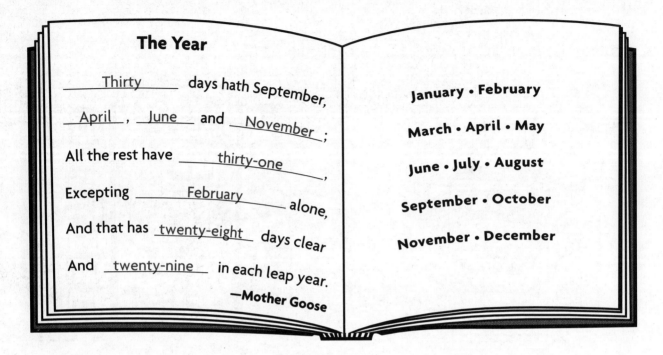

The Year

<u>Thirty</u> days hath September,

<u>April</u> , <u>June</u> and <u>November</u> ;

All the rest have <u>thirty-one</u> ,

Excepting <u>February</u> alone,

And that has <u>twenty-eight</u> days clear

And <u>twenty-nine</u> in each leap year.

—Mother Goose

January • February

March • April • May

June • July • August

September • October

November • December

The Leap Year

Most years have 365 days. But *leap years* have 366 days. The extra day in a leap year is on February 29. Which years are leap years?

- Normally, leap years come every four years. So 1984, 1988, and 1992 were leap years.

- Most century years are *not* leap years. So 1700, 1800, and 1900 were not leap years.

- But every *fourth century year* is a leap year! So 1600, 2000, and 2400 are leap years.

2. Write the next 5 leap years.

1984, 1988, 1992, __**1996**__ , __**2000**__ , __**2004**__ , __**2008**__ , __**2012**__

3. In what year were you born? Was it a leap year? **Answers will vary.**

4. When is the next leap year? _____ **2000 or 2004 or 2008**

Harcourt Brace School Publishers

Find the Figure

Play this game with a partner. You will each need
2 different-colored crayons. **Check students' figures.**

- Each player draws figures *A, B,
  C,* and *D* on his or her grid using
  1 color crayon. Keep the paper
  out of view of the other player.

- Players take turns guessing ordered
  pairs that name points that are part
  of the other player's figures.

- A player that correctly identifies a
  point that is part of one of the other
  player's figures takes another turn.

- Players use the other color crayon
  and the information they get each
  turn to draw their partner's figures
  onto their grid.

- The first player to draw his or her partner's
  figures in their exact locations, wins.

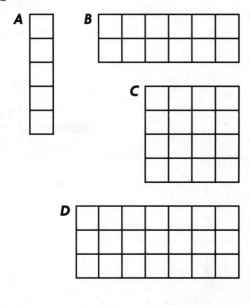

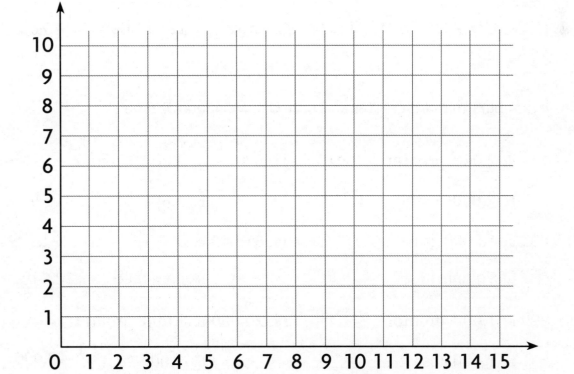

Harcourt Brace School Publishers

Operation: Numbers

How can you change the number
2,744 to 2,044 in one step?

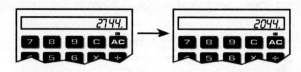

Subtract 700.

Use a calculator. Tell how you can change one number to the
other in one step.

1. 3,825 → 3,805

   __subtract 20__

2. 1,649 → 649

   __subtract 1,000__

3. 4,646 → 4,006

   __subtract 640__

4. 21,715 → 20,715

   __subtract 1,000__

5. 93,686 → 93,286

   __subtract 400__

6. 57,237 → 50,007

   __subtract 7,230__

7. 4,823 → 4,826

   __add 3__

8. 1,335 → 1,835

   __add 500__

9. 8,231 → 9,231

   __add 1,000__

10. 77,123 → 77,723

    __add 600__

11. 50,234 → 50,555

    __add 321__

12. 14,695 → 14,700

    __add 5__

Find the numbers that are greater and less. Use a calculator when
it helps.

13. 6,314 a. 2,000 greater __8,314__

    b. 2,000 less __4,314__

14. 5,967 a. 5,000 greater __10,967__

    b. 5,000 less __967__

15. 16,802 a. 10,000 greater __26,802__

    b. 10,000 less __6,802__

16. 81,043 a. 500 greater __81,543__

    b. 500 less __80,543__

17. 99,999 a. 1,000 greater __100,999__

    b. 1,000 less __98,999__

18. 20,000 a. 1,000 greater __21,000__

    b. 1,000 less __19,000__

Harcourt Brace School Publishers

Which Way to the Summit?

In the White Mountains of New Hampshire there is a range of mountains known as the Presidentials. Many of the mountains in this range have been named after United States presidents.

Write each elevation as a number.

1. Mt. Adams – five thousand, seven hundred seventy-four feet __**5,774 ft**__

2. Mt. Eisenhower – four thousand, seven hundred sixty-one feet __**4,761 ft**__

3. Mt. Franklin – five thousand, four feet __**5,004 ft**__

4. Mt. Jackson – four thousand, fifty-two feet __**4,052 ft**__

5. Mt. Jefferson – five thousand, seven hundred twelve feet __**5,712 ft**__

6. Mt. Madison – five thousand, three hundred sixty-seven feet __**5,367 ft**__

7. Mt. Monroe – five thousand, three hundred eighty-four feet __**5,384 ft**__

8. Mt. Pierce – four thousand, three hundred ten feet __**4,310 ft**__

9. Mt. Washington – six thousand, two hundred eighty-eight feet __**6,288 ft**__

10. Mt. Webster – three thousand, nine hundred ten feet __**3,910 ft**__

Write the names of the mountains in order from greatest elevation to least elevation.

11. **Mt. Washington**	16. **Mt. Franklin**
12. **Mt. Adams**	17. **Mt. Eisenhower**
13. **Mt. Jefferson**	18. **Mt. Pierce**
14. **Mt. Monroe**	19. **Mt. Jackson**
15. **Mt. Madison**	20. **Mt. Webster**

Harcourt Brace School Publishers

Points and Pictures

You will need a ruler.

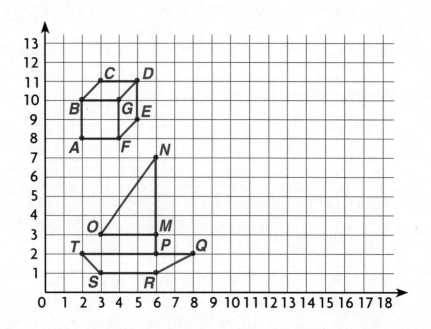

Draw a point (•) at the location of each ordered pair. Label the
point with the letter. Connect the points with straight lines in the
order given. Describe the object you see.

1. A (2,8) B (2,10) C (3,11) D (5,11) E (5,9) F (4,8) G (4,10)
   Connect: A to B to C to D to E to F to G to B to A to F and G to D

   Object: _____ **cube or box** _____

2. M (6,3) N (6,7) O (3,3) P (6,2) Q (8,2) R (6,1) S (3,1) T (2,2)
   Connect: M to N to O to M to P to Q to R to S to T to P

   Object: _____ **sailboat** _____

3. Draw a picture of your own. Write the ordered pair for
   each point. Give directions on how to connect the points.
   Switch papers with a classmate.

   Ordered pairs: _____ **Answers will vary.** _____

   Connect: _____ **Answers will vary.** _____

   Object: _____ **Answers will vary.** _____

Harcourt Brace School Publishers

Name _____

Just Down the Road a Bit

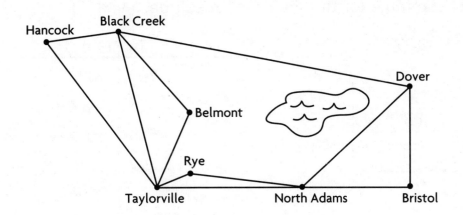

The distance from Taylorville to Rye is 10 miles.

Use the map. Estimate the distances. **Accept answers close to estimates given.**

1. Taylorville to North Adams   **about 40 miles**

2. Hancock to Black Creek   **about 20 miles**

3. Bristol to Dover   **about 25 miles**

4. Belmont to Black Creek   **about 30 miles**

5. Taylorville to Hancock   **about 50 miles**

6. The distance between Taylorville and North Adams is about the same as the distance between what two other towns?

   Taylorville and Black Creek or North Adams and Dover

7. The distance between which two towns is about 2 times as great as the distance between Rye and Taylorville?

   Hancock and Black Creek or Taylorville and Belmont

8. It takes Don longer to bicycle from Bristol to North Adams than to bicycle from Bristol to Dover, although the distance is shorter. Explain why this might be so.

   Possible answer: The terrain is hillier between Bristol

   and North Adams than between Bristol and Dover.

Harcourt Brace School Publishers

STRETCH YOUR THINKING E31

Number Machines

1. Complete the table for this "adding" machine.

In

+ 100

Out

In	Out
700	800
531	**631**
629	**729**
5,102	**5,202**
500	600
2,395	2,495

2. Complete the table for this "subtracting" machine.

In

− 10

Out

In	Out
50	40
65	**55**
543	**533**
1,530	**1,520**
430	420
1,510	1,500

3. Complete the table for this machine. Write what the machine is doing inside the box.

adding 1,000 to each number

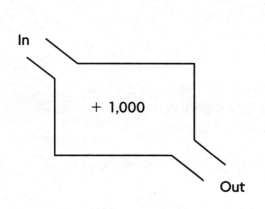

In

+ 1,000

Out

In	Out
4,600	5,600
2,923	**3,923**
43	**1,043**
800	**1,800**
1,100	2,100
4,999	5,999

Harcourt Brace School Publishers

Check It Out

Read each statement below and answer the questions.

1. The Johnson family saved three thousand, five hundred dollars to buy a used car.

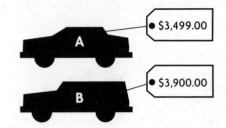

A • $3,499.00

B • $3,900.00

Which car could they afford to buy? _____**A**_____

Why?_____**Possible answer: $3,500 is more than $3,499**_____

2.

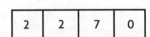

| 2 | 2 | 7 | 0 |

The Johnsons planned to drive two thousand, five hundred seventy miles. When Mrs. Johnson looked at the car odometer, she told her husband they still had three hundred miles to go.

Was she right? _____**yes**_____

Why or why not? _____**2,270 + 300 = 2,570**_____

3.

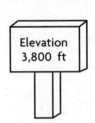

Elevation 3,800 ft

As the Johnsons were driving through a mountain pass, Peter read the sign. He said that they would be more than a mile high if they climbed one thousand, five hundred feet more.

Was he right? _____**yes**_____

Why or why not? _____**Possible answer: 3,800 + 1,500 > 5,280**_____
Remember: 1 mile = 5,280 feet.

4. The Johnsons had decided on a budget of $2,000 before they left on their trip. They spent $150 for gas, $800 for motels, $400 for food, and $325 for repairs and other things.

Did they have any money left when they got home? _____**yes**_____

If so, how much? _____**$325**_____

Harcourt Brace School Publishers

Bank on It

Use play money to help you pay in two different ways for each item pictured below. Write how many you would need of each bill or coin shown.

1.

2.

3.

<u>60</u>

<u>30</u>

<u>70</u>

<u>6</u>

<u>3</u>

<u>7</u>

Write *true* or *false* for each statement.
Use play money to help you choose your answer.

4. Five dimes are equal to 50 pennies. _____**true**_____

5. Seventy pennies are equal to 7 dimes. _____**true**_____

6. Two dollars are equal to 200 dimes. _____**false**_____

7. Four $10 bills are equal to $400. _____**false**_____

8. Ninety dimes are equal to 90 pennies. _____**false**_____

9. Three $1 bills are equal to 30 dimes. _____**true**_____

10. Five hundred dimes are equal to five $10 bills. _____**true**_____

11. Three $100 bills are equal to thirty $10 bills. _____**true**_____

12. Twelve $1 bills are equal to 120 pennies. _____**false**_____

13. Ten $10 bills are equal to one $100 bill. _____**true**_____

Harcourt Brace School Publishers

Spin That Number

Work Together

Use a pencil and a paper clip to make a spinner like the one shown.

Play this game with a partner. Each player spins the paper clip six times. The player's score is the number that the paper clip points to. The other player keeps score, using tally marks.

After each round, find the total value for each player. The player with the higher value wins. Play three rounds. **Totals will vary.**

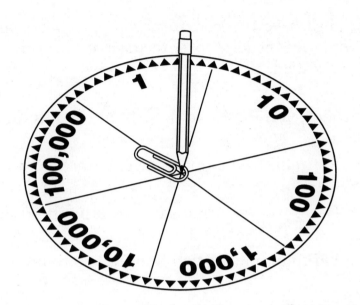

Sample Scorecard							
Name	100,000	10,000	1,000	100	10	1	Total Value
Lu		/	//	//		/	12,201
Miguel	//		/	/	/	/	201,111 winner

1.

Scorecard							
Name	100,000	10,000	1,000	100	10	1	Total Value

2.

3.

4. What is the highest possible total value per round? ___600,000___

Harcourt Brace School Publishers

STRETCH YOUR THINKING   E35

Name _____

LESSON
6.5

Broken Records

Read each world record for the largest collection. Write the missing digit.
Then place the letter over the digit at the bottom of the page to answer
the question.

1. Ties: ten thousand, four hundred fifty-three   10,4__5__3. (W)

2. Refrigerator magnets: twelve thousand   1__2__,000. (A)

3. Pens: fourteen thousand, four hundred ninety-two   1__4__, 492. (G)

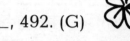

4. Parking meters: two hundred sixty-nine   26__9__. (S)

5. Get-well cards: thirty-three million   3__3__,000,000. (M)

6. Four-leaf clovers: seven thousand, one hundred sixteen

__7__,116. (R)

7. Earrings: eighteen thousand, seven hundred fifty   __1__8,750. (U)

8. Credit cards: one thousand, three hundred eighty-four

1,3__8__4. (P)

9. Soda bottles: six thousand, five hundred ten   __6__, 510. (E)

10. Miniature bottles: twenty nine thousand, five hundred eight

29,5__0__8. (B)

11. What does John collect?

B	U	B	B	L	E		G	U	M		W	R	A	P	P	E	R	S
0	1	0	0		6		4	1	3		5	7	2	8	8	6	7	9

Harcourt Brace School Publishers

Sun to Planet

For Exercises 1–7, use the table.

Planet	Distance from the Sun in Miles
Mercury	36,000,000
Venus	67,000,000
Earth	93,000,000
Mars	141,000,000
Jupiter	486,000,000
Saturn	892,000,000

1. Which two planets are closest together?

   Venus and Earth

2. Which planet is about twice as far from the sun as Mercury is?

   Venus

3. What is the distance between Earth and Saturn?

   799,000,000 mi

4. Which planet is closest to Earth?

   Venus

5. Which planet is closest to Jupiter?

   Mars

6. Which two planets are 856 million miles apart?

   Mercury and Saturn

7. Which planet is about ten times as far from the sun as Earth is?

   Saturn

Harcourt Brace School Publishers

Number Riddles

Use a number line to help answer these number riddles.

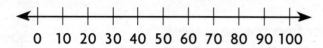

0 10 20 30 40 50 60 70 80 90 100

1. I am greater than 20 and less than 30. I am a multiple

   of 5. ___25___

2. I am less than 80 and greater than 60. The sum of my

   digits is 8. I am even. ___62___

3. I am between 20 and 40. The sum of my digits is 6.

   I am odd. ___33___

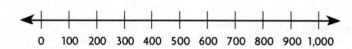

0 100 200 300 400 500 600 700 800 900 1,000

4. I am less than 500 and greater than 400. All my digits

   are the same. ___444___

5. I am between 300 and 400. The sum of my digits is 5.

   I am odd. ___311___

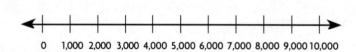

0 1,000 2,000 3,000 4,000 5,000 6,000 7,000 8,000 9,000 10,000

6. I am greater than 1,000 and less than 2,000. The sum

   of my digits is 4. None of my digits is zero. ___1,111___

7. I am between 2,000 and 3,000. I look the same if you
   read me forward or backward. The digit in my tens

   place is 8. ___2,882___

8. Make up your own number riddle. Give enough clues so

   there can be only one answer. __Check students' work.__

Harcourt Brace School Publishers

Number Game

The object of this game is to create a number that is less than your partner's number.

- Make a set of number cards like the ones below. Place them in a pile face down.

- Each player in turn takes a number card and places it on any open space on his or her number board. Once a number card is placed, it cannot be moved. Continue until all the spaces on the number boards are filled.

- The winner is the player with the lesser number. Write the winner's name on the scorecard after each round.

Variation: For each round of this game, take turns deciding if the winner will be the player with the lesser number or the greater number.

0	0	1	1	2	2	3
3	4	4	5	5	6	6
7	7	8	8	9	9	

Number Board   Player 1

Thousands	Hundreds	Tens	Ones

Answers will vary.

Number Board   Player 2

Thousands	Hundreds	Tens	Ones

Round	Winner
1	
2	
3	
4	
5	
6	
7	

Harcourt Brace School Publishers

Check Out the Clues

1. Read the clues to decide how many tickets each class sold. Use the table to help you track your clues. When you find a match, make a check mark.

   • Mr. Ling's class sold fewer than 2,000 tickets.

   • Ms. Finnegan's class sold 1,000 more tickets than Mr. Ling's class.

   • Mr. Park's class sold 10 fewer tickets than Ms. Finnegan's class.

   • Mr. Park's class sold 100 fewer tickets than Mrs. Reed's class.

	2,180	2,280	1,180	2,270	2,170
Mr. Ling			✓		
Ms. Finnegan	✓				
Mrs. Reed				✓	
Mr. Spofford		✓			
Mr. Park					✓

How many tickets did Mr. Spofford's class sell? <u>**2,280 tickets**</u>

2. Make up your own *Check Out the Clues* problem. You choose the topic. Write clues and fill in the table to check your work. **Check students' work.**

   • _____

   • _____

   • _____

Harcourt Brace School Publishers

In Between

In Problems 1–8, fill in the blanks by choosing one of the numbers from the box.

1,335	5,160	57	40
349	498	12	15,721
5,289	15,460	1,672	4,900
3,456	572	1,020	365
29	50	43	15,440

1. Heights of children in inches: 48 < __**50**__ < 52

2. Heights of buildings in feet: 1,535 > __**1,335**__ > 1,025

3. Temperatures in degrees Celsius: 25 < __**29**__ < 36

4. Populations of towns: 15,450 < __**15,460**__ < 15,490

5. Lengths of tunnels in feet: 5,280 > __**5,160**__ > 5,046

6. Ages of trees in years: 241 < __**349**__ < 356

7. Lengths of rivers in miles: 3,710 > __**3,456**__ > 2,980

8. Numbers of stamps in collections: 490 < __**498**__ < 563

In Problems 9–14, circle the number that is between the greatest number and the least number.

9. Ages of grandparents: (61) 72 60

10. Depths of lakes in feet: (328) 230 390

11. Heights of mountains in feet: 20,320 14,573 (14,730)

12. Heights of volcanic eruptions in feet: 9,991 (9,175) 9,003

13. Numbers of Kennel Club collies registered: 14,025 14,281 (14,073)

14. Highest recorded Alaska temperatures: 107 (112) 115

Harcourt Brace School Publishers

Taller or Tallest

For Problems 1–15, use the table.

Mountains in the United States	Height in Feet
Marcy	5,344 ft
Washington	6,288 ft
Guadalupe	8,751 ft
Harney	7,242 ft
Black Mountain	4,145 ft
Olympus	7,965 ft
Mitchell	6,684 ft
Katahdin	5,268 ft

Put these mountains in order from the shortest to the tallest.

1. __Black Mountain__ 2. __Katahdin__

3. __Marcy__ 4. __Washington__

5. __Mitchell__ 6. __Harney__

7. __Olympus__ 8. __Guadalupe__

Write < or > in the ◯ to complete each problem.

9. Katahdin ⟨<⟩ Marcy 10. Olympus ⟨>⟩ Washington

11. Harney ⟨<⟩ Guadalupe 12. Mitchell ⟨>⟩ Black Mountain

13. Guadalupe is more than twice as tall as __Black Mountain__.

14. One mile = 5,280 feet. Which mountain in the table is

closest to one mile high? __Katahdin__

15. Martin climbed about halfway up Mount Washington
with his father. About how high did they climb?

__3,144 ft or about 3,000 ft__

Harcourt Brace School Publishers

Pling-Plop!

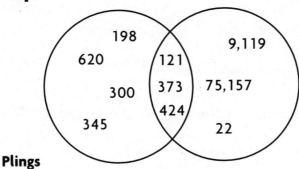

Plings   **Plops**

Study the Venn diagram to help you answer Problems 1–6.

1. Circle the numbers that are Plings.

4,123   (134)   (545)   12   1,467   (367)

2. How would you describe a Pling?

_____**Possible answer: A Pling is a 3-digit number.**_____

3. Circle the numbers that are Plops.

(45,054) (343)   147   (22)   8,568   34,123

4. How would you describe a Plop?

_____**Possible answer: A Plop reads the same backward**_____

and forward.

5. Write four numbers that are both Plings and Plops.

Check students' work.

6. Make up your own version of Pling-Plop numbers.
Answers will vary.

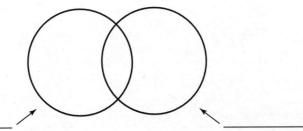

Harcourt Brace School Publishers

Stop That Watch!

Work with a partner to estimate and then check how many times you can do different activities in one minute.

You need a watch with a second hand.

1. Record your estimates and findings in the tables. **Answers will vary.**

Partner 1 Name _____   Partner 2 Name _____

Activity	Estimated Number of Repetitions	Actual Number of Repetitions
Write your name.		
Hop on one foot.		
Draw a star and color it.		
Walk around your desk or table.		
Count to 200.		

Activity	Estimated Number of Repetitions	Actual Number of Repetitions
Write your name.		
Hop on one foot.		
Draw a star and color it.		
Walk around your desk or table.		
Count to 200.		

2. How close are the actual numbers to your estimated numbers? Write a paragraph to explain. **Answers will vary.**

_____

_____

_____

_____

_____

Harcourt Brace School Publishers

What Time Is It?

Each clock shows a time in the morning or the afternoon. Each clock has a letter that you will use to find the secret message.

1. Find the clock that matches each time written below. The times are written as shown on a 24-hour clock. Place the letter of the clock in the box above each

   time. What is the secret message? _____ **time for a party** _____

T	I	M	E
1300	2100	1400	0900

F	O	R
2300	0700	1600

A
1700

P	A	R	T	Y
0400	2 hours before 1900	1 hour after 1500	1 hour after noon	1100

2. Use the letters above the clocks at the top of the page to write the longest word you can in the spaces below. Also write the time for each letter. **Answers will vary.**

Harcourt Brace School Publishers

Replace the Batteries

Mr. Smith went into his clock shop on Monday morning.
Several of his clocks were running slow. He realized that
he needed to replace the batteries in these clocks and reset
the time.

**The exact time is 8:10. Write how much time each clock has lost.
Use the abbreviations *hr* and *min*.**

1.

_____3 hr 5 min_____

2.

_____45 min_____

3.

_____1 hr 42 min_____

4.

_____5 min_____

5.

_____19 min_____

6.

_____3 hr_____

7.

_____3 hr 58 min_____

8.

_____4 hr 44 min_____

Harcourt Brace School Publishers

Time Those Zones!

When it is 7:00 A.M. in San Francisco, it is 10:00 A.M. in New York. That is because the world is divided into time zones.

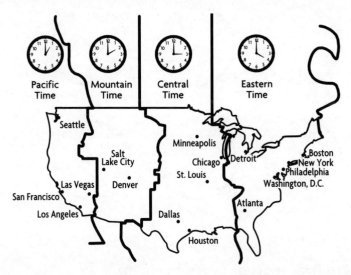

Write the name of the time zone where each city is located.

1. Seattle _____**Pacific**_____   2. Boston _____**Eastern**_____

3. Dallas _____**Central**_____   4. Denver _____**Mountain**_____

For Problems 5–7, use the map of time zones.

5. Tyler lives in Dallas. His cousin Anne lives in Boston. Tyler calls Anne at 4:00 P.M. What time is it in Boston?

    _____**5:00 P.M.**_____

6. An airplane leaves Washington, D.C., at 10:15 A.M. and flies to Detroit. The length of the flight is 1 hour and 45 minutes. What time does the airplane arrive in Detroit?

    _____**12:00 P.M.**_____

7. An airplane leaves New York at 7:00 A.M. and flies to San Francisco. The length of the flight is 6 hours. What time does the airplane arrive in San Francisco?

    _____**10:00 A.M.**_____

Harcourt Brace School Publishers

Name _____

Patterns in Time

Look for a pattern. Draw the hands on the last two clocks.

1.

2.

Write the times to complete the patterns.

3.   12:00   12:05   12:10   **12:15**   **12:20**   **12:25**   **12:30**

4.   7:12   10:12   1:12   **4:12**   **7:12**   **10:12**   **1:12**

5.   1:00   2:15   3:30   4:45   **6:00**   **7:15**   **8:30**

Solve.

6. Bill works at the science museum on Saturdays. He gives a live demonstration with a snake every 45 minutes. The first demonstration is at 10:00 A.M. The last demonstration is at 1:00 P.M. List the start time of each snake demonstration.

     10:00 A.M., 10:45 A.M., 11:30 A.M., 12:15 P.M., 1:00 P.M.

7. Tania displays a turtle and gives a talk every 40 minutes. The talks begin at 10:00 A.M. and end at 12:40 P.M. List the start time of each turtle demonstration.

     10:00 A.M., 10:40 A.M., 11:20 A.M., 12:00 P.M., 12:40 P.M.

8. Peter and his friend arrived at the science museum at 1:15 P.M. His sister will pick them up at 3:00 P.M. How long does Peter have to spend at the museum?

     1 hr 45 min

Harcourt Brace School Publishers

Hatching Eggs

The table shows the average incubation time for eggs of different types of birds. Incubation time is the number of days between the time an egg is laid and the time it hatches.

INCUBATION TIME FOR EGGS	
Kind of Bird	**Average Number of Days**
Chicken	21
Duck	30
Turkey	26
Goose	30

For Problems 1–6, use the table and a calendar.

1. How much longer does it usually take a duck's egg to hatch than a chicken's egg? _____**9 days**_____

2. If a chicken lays an egg on June 1, about what date should the egg hatch? ___**about June 22**___

3. If a duck lays an egg on June 21, about what date should the egg hatch? ___**about July 21**___

4. A turkey egg hatches on July 4. About what date was the turkey egg laid? ___**about June 8**___

5. A goose egg hatches on the last day in July. About what date was the goose egg laid? ___**about July 1**___

6. A chick is 3 days old on July 31. What date did the chicken egg hatch?___**July 28**___

   About what date was the egg laid? ___**about July 7**___

Harcourt Brace School Publishers

Find the Missing Data

The Lane family drove their car on vacation. At the end of each day, Mr. Lane recorded the number of miles that they had driven so far on their trip.

1. About how far did the Lanes travel each day? Complete the table to find out.

Day	Miles in One Day	Total Miles (Cumulative Frequency)
Monday	150 mi	150 miles
Tuesday	75 mi	225 miles
Wednesday	143 mi	368 miles
Thursday	10 mi	378 miles
Friday	122 mi	500 miles
Saturday	75 mi	575 miles

Matt Lane took a notebook on the trip. He used the notebook to draw pictures and play games with his sister.

2. Look at the table below. How many notebook pages did

Matt use by the end of the trip? _____80 pages_____

3. How many pages did Matt use on each day of the trip? Complete the table to find out.

Day	Pages in One Day	Total Pages (Cumulative Frequency)
Monday	20 pages	20 pages
Tuesday	13 pages	33 pages
Wednesday	12 pages	45 pages
Thursday	28 pages	73 pages
Friday	7 pages	80 pages
Saturday	0 pages	80 pages

Harcourt Brace School Publishers

What's for Lunch?

The campers at Hill Camp made their own sandwiches on Friday. Each could choose one kind of bread and one sandwich filling.

The table below shows the kinds of sandwiches that the 20 campers made.

Bread

Filling		Wheat	White	Oatmeal
	Peanut Butter	ⵌⵌ	//	//
	Tuna	///		//
	Cheese	/	/	
	Ham	//	/	/

1. How many campers had ham on oatmeal bread? _____ **1 camper**

2. What kind of sandwich did the most campers make?

   _____ **peanut butter on wheat** _____

3. What kinds of sandwiches did no one make?

   _____ **tuna on white, cheese on oatmeal** _____

4. How many campers used wheat bread to make sandwiches?

   _____ **11 campers** _____

5. Which bread did the most campers choose? _____ **wheat** _____

6. Which sandwich filling did the most campers choose? _____ **peanut butter**

7. How many kinds of sandwiches can the campers make? _____ **12 kinds**

8. If the camp offered one more kind of bread, how many kinds

   of sandwiches could the campers make? _____ **16 kinds** _____

Harcourt Brace School Publishers

Coin Combos

Samantha wants to buy a granola bar from the snack machine. The granola bar costs $0.45. The machine takes only quarters, nickels, and dimes. It does not give change.

1. Use the table to list all the ways that Samantha can put $0.45 into the snack machine.

Quarters	Dimes	Nickels		Total
1 × 25	2 × 10	0 × 5	=	$0.45
1 × 25	1 × 10	2 × 5	=	$0.45
1 × 25	0 × 10	4 × 5	=	$0.45
0 × 25	4 × 10	1 × 5	=	$0.45
0 × 25	3 × 10	3 × 5	=	$0.45
0 × 25	2 × 10	5 × 5	=	$0.45
0 × 25	1 × 10	7 × 5	=	$0.45
0 × 25	0 × 10	9 × 5	=	$0.45

2. What is the least number of coins Samantha could use? __**3 coins**__

3. What is the greatest number of coins Samantha could use? __**9 coins**__

Another snack machine gives change in quarters, dimes, or nickels if more than the exact amount is put into the machine.

4. Samantha puts 2 quarters into the machine to buy a

   $0.45 granola bar. What will her change be? __**$0.05**__

5. Samantha puts a $1 bill into the machine to buy a

   $0.45 granola bar. What will her change be? __**$0.55**__

6. List two ways the machine could give $0.55 in change.

   __**Possible answers: two quarters, one nickel; five dimes, one nickel.**__

Harcourt Brace School Publishers

The Case of the Missing Tallies

Joe took a survey to find out what kinds of books his classmates like best. He wrote the survey results in a frequency
table. Then he wrote down these survey facts:

- The same number of students like books about
  inventions and books about science best.

- Twice as many students like mystery books better
  than science books.

- Biography books are liked by the fewest students.

- An odd number of students like adventure books best.

- More students like animal books better than sports
  books.

Joe made a puzzle for his classmates. He cut out the tally
boxes from his frequency table and mixed them up.

/	⊬⊬⊬	///	⊬⊬⊬ /	////	///	//

Use the survey facts to find out where each group of tally
marks belongs. Make copies or cut out the tally boxes
shown. Move the tally boxes around on the frequency table
until you find an arrangement that matches the survey facts.
Write the totals in the last column.

FAVORITE TYPES OF BOOKS

Type of Book	Tally	Total
Adventure	⊬⊬⊬	5
Animals	////	4
Mystery	⊬⊬⊬ /	6
Inventions	///	3
Biography	/	1
Science	///	3
Sports	//	2

Harcourt Brace School Publishers

Clue to the Ages

1. Use the clues to fill in the names of the people on the bar graph.

   Clues:

   • Hannah is 7 years older than Josh.

   • Carolyn is twice as old as Josh.

   • Sandra is younger than Carolyn.

   • Kyle is older than Andrew.

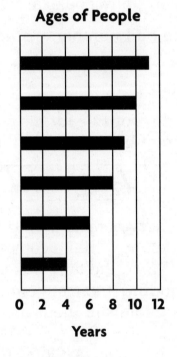

Ages of People

Names

Hannah

Kyle

Andrew

Carolyn

Sandra

Josh

0 2 4 6 8 10 12
Years

2. Use the following information to draw bars on the graph below.

   Clues:

   • Stephanie is one year younger than Cory.

   • Stephanie is twice as old as Scott.

   • Scott is one year older than Tim.

   • Tim is 3 years old.

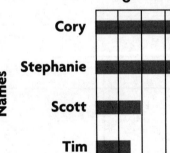

Ages of People

Names

Cory

Stephanie

Scott

Tim

0 2 4 6 8 10 12
Years

Harcourt Brace School Publishers

Did You Know?

The table shows the oldest recorded age of some animals.

Animal	Age (in years)
Cat	28 yrs
Dog	20 yrs
Goat	18 yrs
Rabbit	13 yrs
Guinea Pig	8 yrs
Mouse	6 yrs

Use data in the table above to complete the graph. Draw bars across the graph to show the age of each animal.

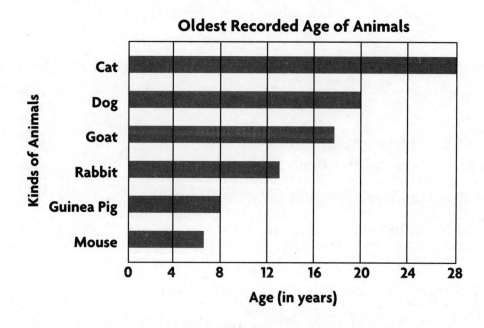

1. What interval is used in the scale of the graph?

_____ 4 _____

2. For which animals do the bars end exactly on the scale lines?

_____ **cat, dog, guinea pig** _____

3. If the graph had a scale with intervals of 2, how many bars would end exactly on the scale lines?

_____ **5 bars** _____

Harcourt Brace School Publishers

Name _____

Strike Up the Band

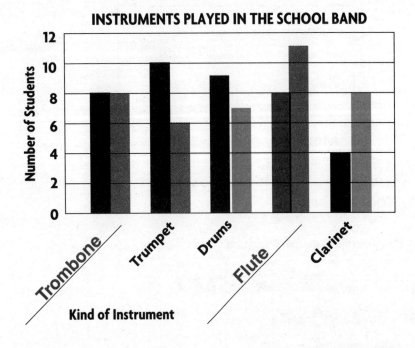

INSTRUMENTS PLAYED IN THE SCHOOL BAND

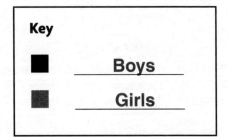

Key

■ _____ **Boys** _____

■ _____ **Girls** _____

1. Use the clues to fill in the missing information on this double-bar graph. **Check students' graphs.**

   • The same number of boys and girls play the trombone.

   • More boys than girls play the trumpet.

   • Two more boys than girls play the drums.

   • More girls play the flute than any other instrument.

   • The same number of boys play the flute and the trombone.

   • Twice as many girls as boys play the clarinet.

For Problems 2–5, use the completed graph.

2. Which instruments are played by more boys than girls?

   _____ **trumpet and drums** _____

3. Do more students play the flute or the trumpet? ____ **flute** ____

4. Are there more boys or more girls in the band? ____ **more girls** ____

5. How many students are in the band? _____ **79** _____

Harcourt Brace School Publishers

Temperature Patterns

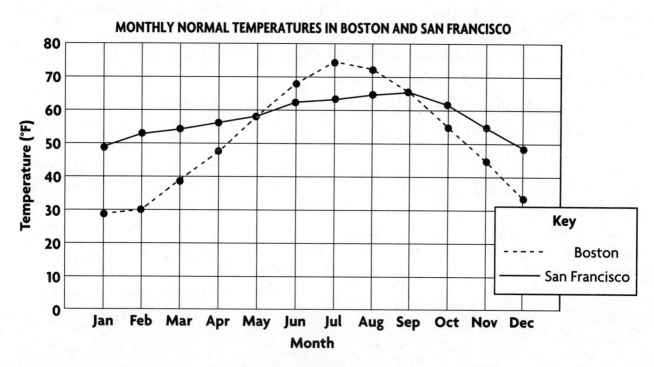

MONTHLY NORMAL TEMPERATURES IN BOSTON AND SAN FRANCISCO

Key
- - - - - Boston
——— San Francisco

This line graph shows the normal temperatures in
Boston and San Francisco for each month of the year.

1. What does the dashed line represent?

   normal temperatures in Boston

2. What is normally the coldest month in Boston?

   January

3. What is normally the warmest month in San Francisco?

   September

4. In which city is the difference in temperature between
   the summer months and the winter months greater?

   Boston

5. During which months is the normal temperature in the
   two cities the same?

   May and September

Harcourt Brace School Publishers

STRETCH YOUR THINKING   E57

What's in a Name?

Stephanie is comparing the number of letters in her classmates' first names. She printed each student's name on a piece of paper. She then began to count and record the number of letters in each name.

1. Complete Stephanie's line plot by recording the number of letters in the first names of the other students in her class.

Jennifer	Zachary	Lee	Elizabeth	Dimitri
Ted	Inderjeet	Trudi	Malcolm	Lauren
Carl	Koko	Matthew	Moe	Kathleen
Juan	Joanie	Christopher	Oscar	Ramona
Paul	Siri	Mercedes	Kevin	Alan

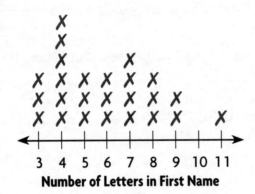

Number of Letters in First Name

For Problems 2–5, use the completed line plot.

2. How many students have 7 letters in their first name?

4 students

3. What is the most common number of letters for a first

   name in Stephanie's class? _____ **4 letters** _____

4. What is the range in this data? _____ **8** _____

5. Would the data be different if you made a line plot for the number of letters in the first names of students in your class? Make a list of names and a line plot for your classmates.

   Yes; Check students' work.

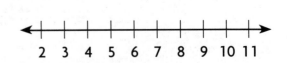

Harcourt Brace School Publishers

How Many Marbles in a Jar?

Mr. Murphy asked each of the students in his class to estimate the number of marbles in a jar. He organized the estimates in a stem-and-leaf plot.

Marble Estimates

Stem	Leaves
6	3 5 5 6 7
7	0 0 0 4 4 5 8 9 9
8	0 3 3 6 6
9	0 5

For Problems 1–4, use the stem-and-leaf plot.

1. What number was estimated by most students?

   _____ 70 _____

2. What is the middle number in this set of estimates?

   _____ 75 _____

3. What is the difference between the highest estimate and

   the lowest estimate? _____ 32 _____

4. Use the following clues and the stem-and-leaf plot to determine the exact number of marbles in the jar.

   • Only one student guessed the exact number.

   • The exact number is not a multiple of 5.

   • The exact number has 7 tens.

   There are exactly _____ 78 _____ marbles in the jar.

Harcourt Brace School Publishers

Data Display

Corina recorded the grades that she got on her spelling test each week for nine weeks. She displayed the data in two different ways.

Plot A

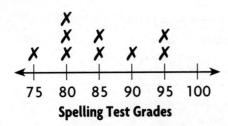

Graph B

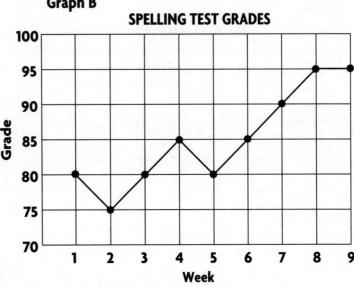

Circle the letter of the graph or plot you would use to answer each question. Then answer the questions.

1. What grade did Corina get most often? (Plot A) Graph B _____ **80**

2. What grade did Corina get in Week 5? Plot A (Graph B) _____ **80**

3. Did Corina's grades improve or decline between Weeks 5 and 9?

   Plot A (Graph B) _____ **improve**

4. What is the range of Corina's grades? Plot A Graph B _____ **20 points**

   _____ **Possible answers: Plot A, Graph B, or both**

5. By how many points did Corina's grade improve between Weeks 2 and 3?

   Plot A (Graph B) _____ **by 5 points**

6. What is the median of Corina's grades? Plot A Graph B _____ **85 points**

   _____ **Possible answers: Plot A, Graph B, or both**

Harcourt Brace School Publishers

Find the Missing Scales

The line graphs below show the number of sales of several items in
The Red Balloon toy shop during one week.

1. Use the following information to fill in the missing scales
   in each graph.
   • There were 10 more puzzles sold on Monday than on Tuesday.
   • The number of models sold on Wednesday was 5.
   • There were 60 paint sets sold during the week.
   • There were 8 more games sold on Thursday than on Friday.

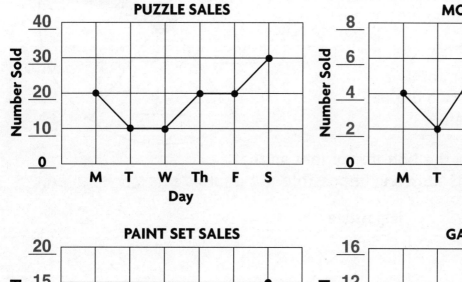
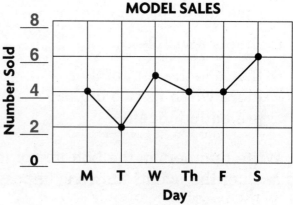
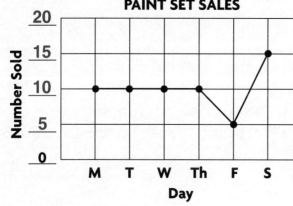

For Problems 2–5, use the graphs.

2. How many models were sold in all during the week? _____ **25 models** _____

3. On which day was the greatest number of paint sets sold? _____ **Saturday** _____

4. Were there more sales of models or games on Monday? _____ **games** _____

5. Write two more similar questions using the data in the graphs.

Check students' questions.

Harcourt Brace School Publishers

Certainly Not!

Remember, if an event is *certain*, it will always happen. If an event is *impossible*, it will never happen.

1. Write numbers in the top spinner so that each of the following events is certain.

   Spinning a number

   A. that is greater than 25

   B. that has 12 as a factor

   C. that is divisible by 3

   D. that has the sum of 8 or more when its two digits are added together

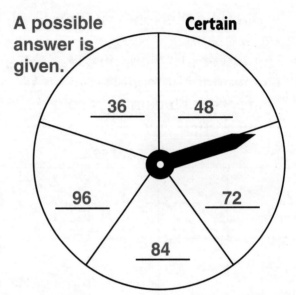

A possible answer is given.

Certain

36   48

96   72

84

2. Write numbers in the bottom spinner so that each of the events above is impossible. **A possible answer is given.**

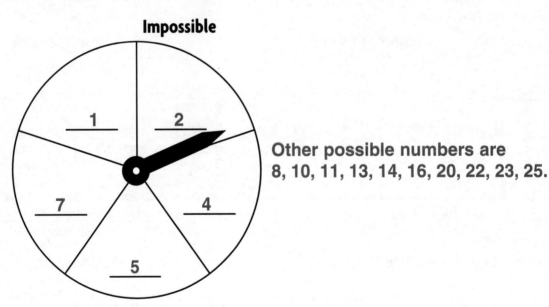

Impossible

1   2

7   4

5

Other possible numbers are
8, 10, 11, 13, 14, 16, 20, 22, 23, 25.

3. Look at the bottom spinner. Write two more events that would be impossible if you were to use the spinner.

   Answers may vary. _____

   _____

Harcourt Brace School Publishers

A Likely Story

A single dart can land anywhere on this dart board. Tell whether each event is *likely* or *unlikely*.

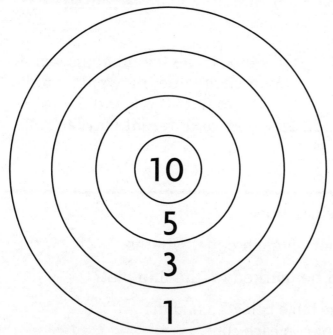

1. The score is an odd number. _____likely_____

2. The score is more than 3. _____unlikely_____

3. The score is 3. _____unlikely_____

4. The score is 1 or 3. _____likely_____

5. The score is less than 10. _____likely_____

6. The dart lands exactly in the center of the board. _____unlikely_____

7. The dart hits the number 3. _____unlikely_____

8. The score is 1, 3, or 10. _____likely_____

9. The score is greater than 1. _____likely_____

10. The score is 5. _____unlikely_____

11. The score is 10. _____unlikely_____

12. The dart lands inside the zero in the number 10. _____unlikely_____

Harcourt Brace School Publishers

Name _____

Mystery Cube

Yancy wrote 6 one-digit numbers on a cube. Then he made
an identical cube. The line plot shows the sums and the
number of ways he could roll each sum if he were to roll his
two number cubes.

? + ? = ?

HINT: If Yancy wrote the numbers 4 and
5 on each cube, he would count
rolling 4 + 5 and 5 + 4 as
two different ways to roll.

Use the line plot to answer the question.

1. If 1 were the least number on each cube, what is

   the least sum that would be marked on the line plot? __2__

Use the line plot. Complete the table below to find the
6 one-digit numbers Yancy wrote on each cube.

2.

Sum	Number of Ways to Roll	Ways to Roll
8	1	4 + 4
9	2	4 + 5, 5 + 4
10	3	4 + 6, 6 + 4, 5 + 5
11	4	4 + 7, 7 + 4, 5 + 6, 6 + 5
12	5	4 + 8, 8 + 4, 5 + 7, 7 + 5, 6 + 6
13	6	4 + 9, 9 + 4, 5 + 8, 8 + 5, 6 + 7, 7 + 6
14	5	5 + 9, 9 + 5, 6 + 8, 8 + 6, 7 + 7
15	4	6 + 9, 9 + 6, 7 + 8, 8 + 7
16	3	7 + 9, 9 + 7, 8 + 8
17	2	8 + 9, 9 + 8
18	1	9 + 9

3. The numbers Yancy wrote on each cube are ____4, 5, 6, 7, 8, 9____.

Harcourt Brace School Publishers

Name Mix-up

Read the probabilities given. They describe the chances of picking specific students' names from a bag. Six names were not put into either bag. Use the information to decide which bag each name should go into. Write the correct names on the cards below.

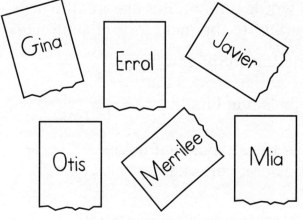

Ms. Simon's Class Bag	**Mrs. Kipp's Class Bag**
The probability of drawing a name	The probability of drawing a name

The probability of drawing a name

a. beginning with a vowel is $\frac{3}{9}$, or $\frac{1}{3}$.

b. ending in the letter l is $\frac{2}{9}$.

c. beginning with the letter J, K, L, or M is $\frac{6}{9}$, or $\frac{2}{3}$.

The probability of drawing a name

a. ending in a vowel is $\frac{5}{9}$.

b. with 5 or more letters is $\frac{3}{9}$, or $\frac{1}{3}$.

c. beginning with the letter V is $\frac{0}{9}$.

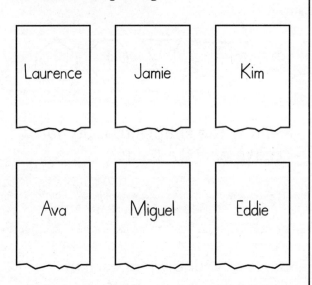

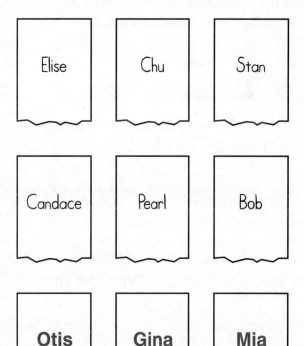

Order of names within each group may vary.

Harcourt Brace School Publishers

Word Wonders

The words *and, or, not* are small words, but they are very important to the meanings of sentences.

Circle the shape that has 4 sides *and* has sides that are the same length.

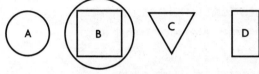

Circle the shapes that have 3 sides *or* a consonant.

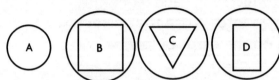

Circle the shapes that are *not* triangles.

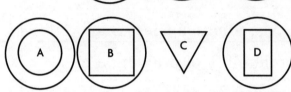

For Problems 1–3, use the shapes at the right.

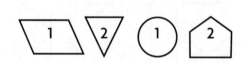

1. Draw the shapes that have exactly 4 sides *and* the number 1.

2. Draw the shapes that are triangles *or* have the number 2.

3. Draw the shapes that do *not* have exactly 4 sides.

Use the shapes with the numbers. Write a sentence of your own for each of the words *and, or, not*. Draw the answer. **Questions will vary. Check students' drawings.**

4. _____

5. _____

6. _____

Harcourt Brace School Publishers

Number Neighbors

When folded into a cube, each of the nets below will
have either the number 1 or the number 2 on each face.

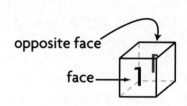

opposite face

face

Predict which of the nets will make cubes on which
the "1" faces will be opposite each other.

Trace each net. Then cut out the tracing, fold, and
tape to form a cube to check your prediction. **Predictions will vary.**

1. Are the "1" faces opposite?

Prediction _____

Check ___yes___

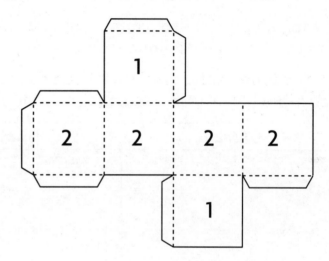

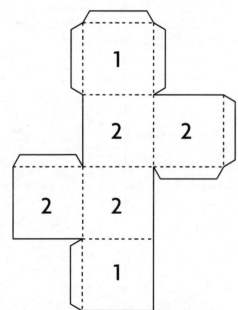

2. Are the "1" faces opposite?

Prediction _____

Check ___no___

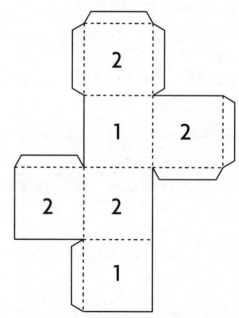

3. Are the "1" faces opposite?

Prediction _____

Check ___yes___

Harcourt Brace School Publishers

The Game of Sprout Figures

Play this game several times with a partner. Each player has a different-colored pencil.

- One player draws 5 points, anywhere on a sheet of paper.

- Take turns connecting one point to another. You cannot cross another line.

- When all 5 points are connected, draw 5 more points. Each new point becomes a part of the game.

- The winner is the player who connects the last possible line. **Check students' drawings.**

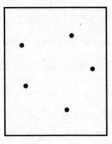

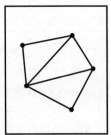

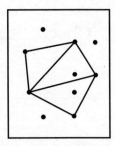

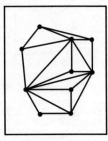

GAME 1	GAME 2
GAME 3	**GAME 4**

Harcourt Brace School Publishers

Puzzle Watch

Here are two puzzles to solve.

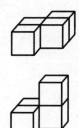

1. A supermarket worker wants to know how many ways he can stack four cube-shaped boxes. He can stack them in 1, 2, 3, or 4 layers. Help by finding as many arrangements as you can. Draw the arrangements below. How many did you find?

Some possible arrangements are shown.

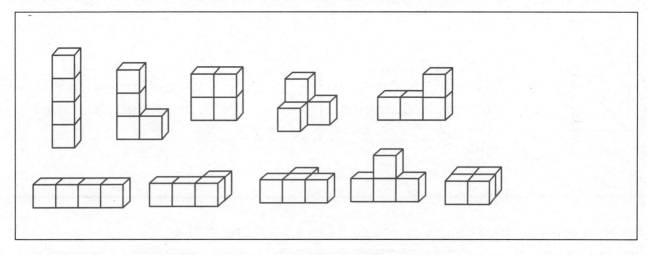

2. Draw five points on a sheet of paper. Make sure no three points are placed in a row. Connect each point to *all* the other points. When you connect the five points, how many triangles can you find in the figure?

Drawings will vary. There are 35 triangles.

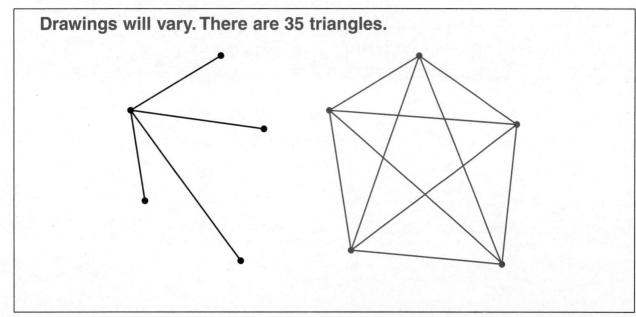

Harcourt Brace School Publishers

Amazing Triangles!

You can make many different figures from 4 right triangles.
Trace and cut out the four triangles below.

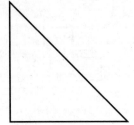 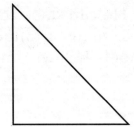 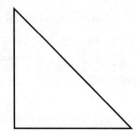 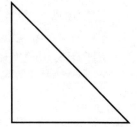

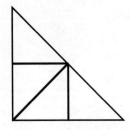
This is a 3-sided figure made from the 4 right triangles.

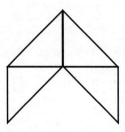
This is a 6-sided figure made from the 4 right triangles.

Make as many 6-sided figures as you can. Draw each one in the box below. **Some possible figures are shown.**

Work Space

    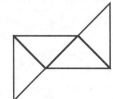

Harcourt Brace School Publishers

Face Off!

These drawings show solid figures viewed from one side.
Name two solid figures that they may be part of.
Possible answers are given.

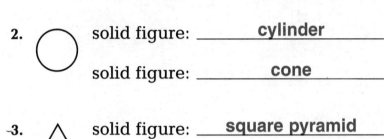

1. solid figure: _____**cube**_____

   solid figure: _____**square pyramid**_____

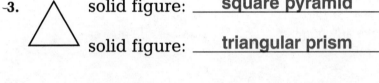

2. solid figure: _____**cylinder**_____

   solid figure: _____**cone**_____

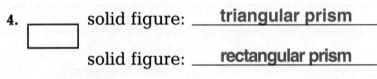

3. solid figure: _____**square pyramid**_____

   solid figure: _____**triangular prism**_____

4. solid figure: _____**triangular prism**_____

   solid figure: _____**rectangular prism**_____

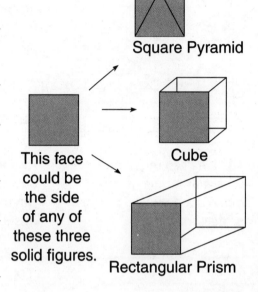

Square Pyramid

This face could be the side of any of these three solid figures.

Cube

Rectangular Prism

Imagine that you traced each face of the solid shown. Draw each
face below.

5.

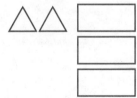

6.

7.

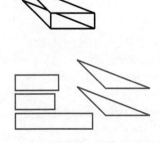

8.

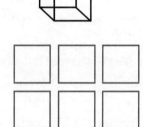

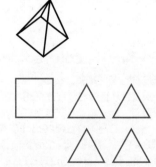

Harcourt Brace School Publishers

Name _____

Checkmate!

The game of chess was invented more than 1,300 years ago. Today it is played in all parts of the world. Each piece has its own ways to move. For example:

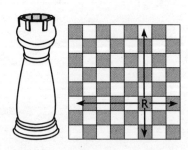

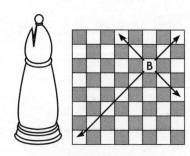

The *king* can move one square at a time. It can move up, down, left, right, or diagonally.

A *rook* can move up, or down, left, or right. It can move any number of squares.

A *bishop* can move diagonally any number of squares.

Solve.

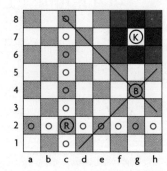

1. Which chess piece is in g4? __bishop__

2. Which piece is in c2? __rook__

3. Can the king move to h6? __yes__

4. Can the bishop move to d8? __no__

The queen is the most powerful chess piece. It can move any number of squares up, down, left, right, or diagonally. Suppose the queen is at b7. Can it move from b7 to each of the following squares? Write *yes* or *no*.

5. d7 __yes__   6. d6 __no__   7. a4 __no__   8. g2 __yes__

For Exercises 9–11, use colored pencils to color squares on the chess board. **Check students' work.**

9. Color blue all the squares to which the king can move. **King's squares are shaded.**

10. Color red all the squares to which the bishop can move. **Bishop's squares have lines drawn through them.**

11. Color yellow all the squares to which the rook can move. **Rook's squares have small circles on them.**

Harcourt Brace School Publishers

Riddle, Riddle

Name the plane or solid figure described by each riddle.

1. When you trace one face of a cone or a cylinder, you see me. What am I?

   a circle

2. I have 6 flat faces that all look exactly the same. What am I?

   a cube

3. You see two sizes of me when you trace a rectangular prism. What am I?

   a rectangle

4. If you trace me six times, you make a cube. What figure am I?

   a square

5. I am a solid figure with one round face. What am I?

   a cone

6. If you trace my 5 faces, you will find a square and triangles. What am I?

   a square pyramid

7. I have as many sides as an octopus has legs. What figure am I?

   an octagon

8. I am a solid figure with no vertices or edges. What am I?

   a sphere

9. I am a solid figure with 4 identical faces that meet at one point. What am I?

   a square pyramid

Harcourt Brace School Publishers

Artworks

You can create artwork.

1. Cut any shape figure with at least one corner from heavy paper or cardboard.

2. Draw a point in the center of your work space.

3. Draw a point on any corner of the figure.

4. Place the corner of the figure on the center point.

5. Trace around the figure.

6. Now, rotate the figure around the same point a small distance. Trace again.

7. Continue rotating and tracing until you return to where you started. Rotate about the same distance each time. Do at least eight rotations.

8. Color your drawing. **Check students' drawings.**

Work Space

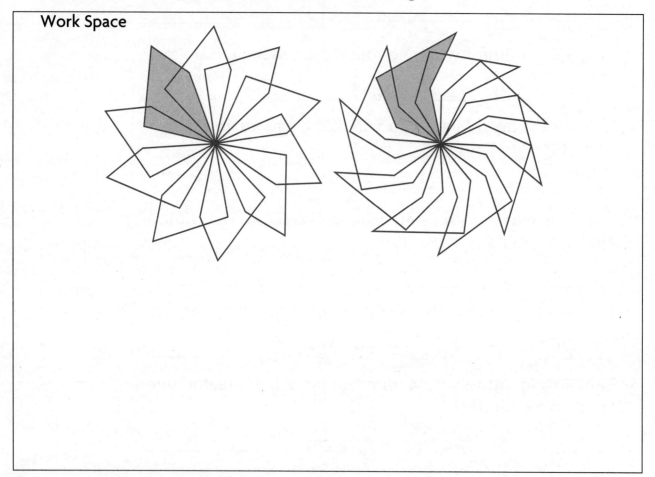

Harcourt Brace School Publishers

Line Up for Fun!

1. Can you solve the following puzzle?

Using the nine points, draw four lines.

You may use each point only once.

You may cross lines.

Each line must be connected.

You may not lift your pencil.

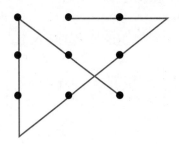

---

2. Connect the pairs of points to make line segments by using a straightedge. A picture will appear.

line segment *AH*	line segment *QS*
line segment *AF*	line segment *TW*
line segment *FH*	line segment *QT*
line segment *AG*	line segment *SW*
line segment *BC*	line segment *RU*
line segment *DE*	line segment *MK*
line segment *BD*	line segment *NL*
line segment *CE*	line segment *MN*
line segment *FI*	line segment *ML*
line segment *HJ*	line segment *KN*
line segment *IJ*	line segment *OP*

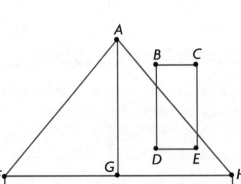
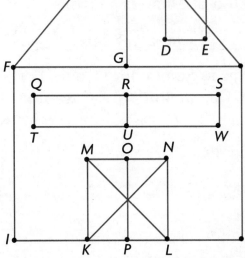

Harcourt Brace School Publishers

STRETCH YOUR THINKING   E75

Name _____

Semaphore Code

The Semaphore Code was used by the United States Navy
to send short-range messages. The message sender holds two
flags in various positions to represent the letters of the alphabet.

To make a number, give the "numeral" sign first. Then use A = 1,
B = 2, C = 3, and so on for the digits 1–9. Use J for zero.

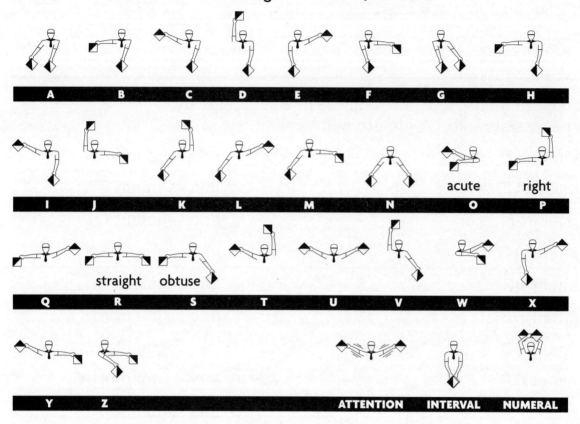

1. The Semaphore Code makes use of angles. Choose a
   letter and explain what kind of angle is shown.

   Answers will vary.

2. Write your name by using the Semaphore Code. For
   example, *Mark* would be **Check students' drawings.**

    All angles shown are obtuse.

   M   A   R   K

3. Now, write the year in Semaphore Code. **Check students' drawings.**

Mapmaker, Mapmaker, Make Me a Map!

Use your knowledge of lines and angles and the following instructions to complete the map. Use a pencil and a straightedge.

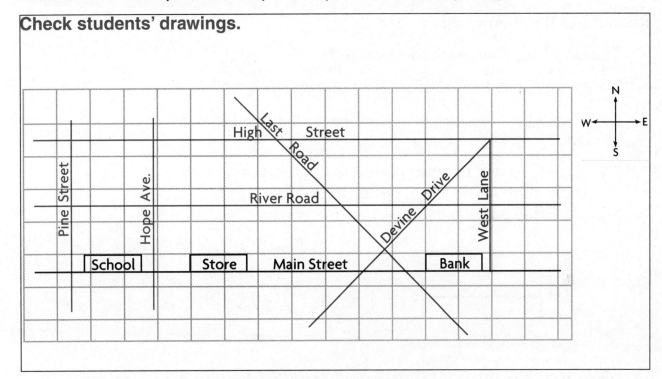

Check students' drawings.

1. Draw River Road to the north of and parallel to Main Street.

2. Draw High Street to the north of and parallel to River Road.

3. Draw West Lane to the east of the bank and perpendicular to Main Street. West Lane is a line segment from Main Street to High Street.

4. Draw Pine Street to the west of the school and perpendicular to River Road.

5. Draw Hope Ave. to the east of the school and west of the store. Hope Ave. is parallel to West Lane.

6. Draw Devine Drive as a ray beginning at the intersection of West Lane and High Street. It moves southwest and intersects Main Street east of the store.

7. Draw Last Road perpendicular to Devine Drive, intersecting Main Street west of the bank.

Harcourt Brace School Publishers

STRETCH YOUR THINKING   E77

Powerful Bars

Help out the athletes by choosing the correct plates to put on the weight-lifting dumbbell bar.

Remember the following:

- The dumbbell bar weighs 45 pounds.

- Plates weigh 5, 10, 25, 35, or 45 pounds.

- A matching plate must be added to both sides to balance the bar.

- It's quicker to use heavier plates. So adding one 10-pound plate to a side is better than adding two 5-pound plates to a side.

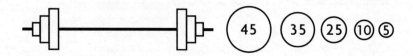

1. Anna wants to lift 135 pounds. Which plates should be used?

Possible answer: two 45-lb plates

2. Anna wants to increase the weight to 185 pounds. Which plates should be added?

Possible answer: two 25-lb plates

3. The world record for the bench press is 765 pounds. Which plates would be needed for such a task?

Possible answer: sixteen 45-lb plates

4. Mark wants to bench press about 300 pounds. What would you suggest he use?

Possible answer: six 45-lb plates

Harcourt Brace School Publishers

Polygons in Art

Modern art is often based on geometric figures.
Here is a sample.

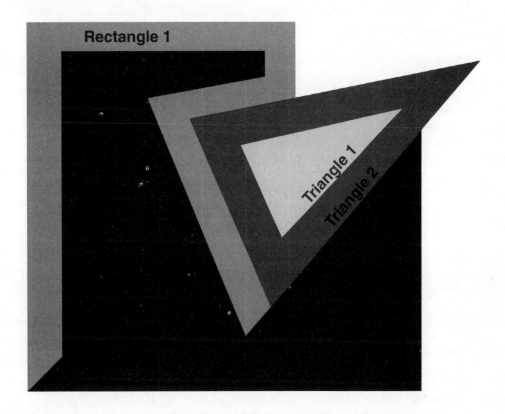

For Problems 1–4, use the sketch.

1. Label the 2 triangles Triangle 1 and Triangle 2. **Check students' work.**

2. Are their angles *acute, obtuse,* or *right*?

   acute

3. Label the grey background rectangle, which is partially covered, Rectangle 1. **Check students' work.**

4. Now, create your own art in this style. Cut geometric shapes from colored paper. Put them together in a creative way. **Check students' work.**

Harcourt Brace School Publishers

A Scavenger Hunt

Quadrilaterals are all around you. Here is your chance
to find them. By yourself or in a small group, find the
shapes listed below. Search for shapes in your classroom,
on the playground, or at home. Use the chart to record
your findings.

Give yourself the following points for each shape.
Challenge yourself to find the harder shapes—and
score more points!

Square	1 point
Rectangle	1 point
Rhombus	2 points
Trapezoids	3 points
Parallelograms	4 points
General Quadrilaterals	5 points

Answers will vary.

Shape Found	Description	Points
rectangle	cafeteria table	1

Harcourt Brace School Publishers

A Special Puzzle

A tangram is a seven-piece puzzle made up of five
triangles, a square, and a parallelogram. The pieces
can be made into more than 7,000 figures and designs.
Trace the tangram below and cut out each piece.

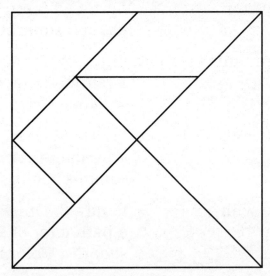

Try these activities, using your tangram pieces. Trace each figure
that you create. **Answers will vary. Check students' work.**

1. Create squares by using various combinations of tangram

   pieces. How many squares can you make? _____

2. Create a rectangle using the following pieces:
   a. 1 square and 2 small triangles
   b. 1 parallelogram and 2 small triangles
   c. 5 triangles

3. Create quadrilaterals from various combinations
   of tangram pieces. How many quadrilaterals can

   you make? _____

4. Create letters of the alphabet from tangram pieces. How

   many letters can you make? _____

5. Create animal figures from tangram pieces. What

   animal figures can you make? _____

6. What other creative figures can you make from

   tangram pieces? _____

Harcourt Brace School Publishers

STRETCH YOUR THINKING E81

Block It Out!

Read the directions for making each figure. Draw, number, and
color the figure on the grid below. **Check students' drawings.
Possible drawings shown.**

1. Figure 1: Draw a square figure
   with a perimeter of 4, using
   1 square. Color it red.

2. Figure 2: Draw a rectangular
   figure with a perimeter of 10,
   using 6 squares. Color it green.

3. Figure 3: Draw a square figure
   with a perimeter of 12, using
   9 squares. Color it blue.

4. Figure 4: Draw a figure with
   a perimeter of 14, using 9
   squares. Color it black.

5. Figure 5: Draw a figure with
   a perimeter of 12, using 5
   squares. Color it yellow.

6. Figure 6: Draw a figure with
   a perimeter of 24, using 11
   squares. Color it purple.

7. Figure 7: Draw a figure with
   a perimeter of 16, using 16
   squares. Color it brown.

8. Figure 8: Draw a figure with
   a perimeter of 20, using 21
   squares. Color it orange.

1 red
2 green
3 blue
4 black
5 yellow
6 purple
7 brown
8 orange

Harcourt Brace School Publishers

Math Is Not a Palindrome!

Words or numbers that read the same forward and
backward are called palindromes. Some examples are
Otto, Hannah, 44, 343, 9119, and the phrase *a man a
plan a canal Panama.*

A number that is not a palindrome can be changed into one.
Just reverse the digits and add. Try the number 13:

$$
\begin{array}{r}
13 \\
+31 \\
\hline
44
\end{array}
\text{ (reversed digits)}
$$

For some numbers, more than one addition is needed. Try the
number 68:

$$
\begin{array}{r}
68 \\
+86 \\
\hline
154 \\
+451 \\
\hline
605 \\
+506 \\
\hline
1,111
\end{array}
\text{ (reversed digits)}
$$

Now you can create palindromes. Try making at least 8 number palindromes based
on the numbers 10 to 99. Record your results and the number of steps needed
on the chart below. Don't try 89 or 98—each takes 24 steps and results in the
palindrome 8,813,200,023,188! **Answers will vary.**

	Number	Steps	Palindrome
1.			
2.			
3.			
4.			
5.			
6.			
7.			
8.			

Harcourt Brace School Publishers

Brand X

Do some paper towels really soak up more water than others? You can do an experiment to find out! You will need three brands of paper towels, a dropper, a transparent square-centimeter grid, and water dyed with food coloring.

Make a Prediction:

1. Which brand of paper towel do you think will soak up the most water?

_____

2. Will using twice as much water cover twice as much area?

_____

The Experiment:

- Lay flat one sheet of each brand of paper towel.

- From about 1 foot high, drip two drops of water on each paper towel.

- Place the transparent square-centimeter grid over each paper towel.

- Record the area of wetness for each sheet.

- Repeat with new towels, using 4 drops of water. Record your results.

	2 Drops Brand ____	2 Drops Brand ____	2 Drops Brand ____	4 Drops Brand ____	4 Drops Brand ____	4 Drops Brand ____
Area That Soaked Up Water (sq cm)						

3. Which paper towel soaked up the most water? Explain your

results. _____ **Accept all reasonable responses.** _____

4. Did twice the amount of water cover twice as much area?

_____ **Answers will vary.** _____

Riddle: What gets wetter and wetter the more it dries? _____ **a towel** _____

Harcourt Brace School Publishers

Unusual Measures

A very long time ago, people used body units to measure lengths.

Span   length from the end of the thumb to the end of the little finger when the hand is stretched fully

Cubit   length from the elbow to the longest finger

Fathom   length from fingertip to fingertip when arms are stretched fully in opposite directions

Pace   length of a walking step, measured from toe of back foot to toe of front foot

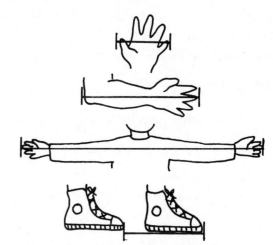

You can use body measures to find the perimeters and areas of objects at school. Record your results in the chart below. **Answers will vary.**

Object Measured	Measured in Spans		Measured in Cubits	
	Perimeter	Area	Perimeter	Area
Desk Top	14 spans	12 sq spans	9 cubits	$4\frac{1}{2}$ sq cubits
1.				
2.				
3.				
4.				

5. Measure the length and the width of your classroom in fathoms and in paces. **Answers will vary.**

length of classroom: _____ fathoms; _____ paces

width of classroom: _____ fathoms; _____ paces

Harcourt Brace School Publishers

Coordinate Tic-Tac-Toe

Try a new twist on the game of tic-tac-toe!

Instead of the traditional grid with nine spaces, you can play on a coordinate grid with more than 100 spaces. In this game, you put your **X** or **O** on the intersection of two lines instead of in the space!

How to play:

1. Use the coordinate grid below.

2. Players (or teams of players) take turns naming coordinate points for **X** and **O.** The points must be named by ordered pairs.

3. Players' marks are placed on the named intersections (not in the spaces).

4. The first player (or team) to get four **X**'s or four **O**'s in a row is the winner!

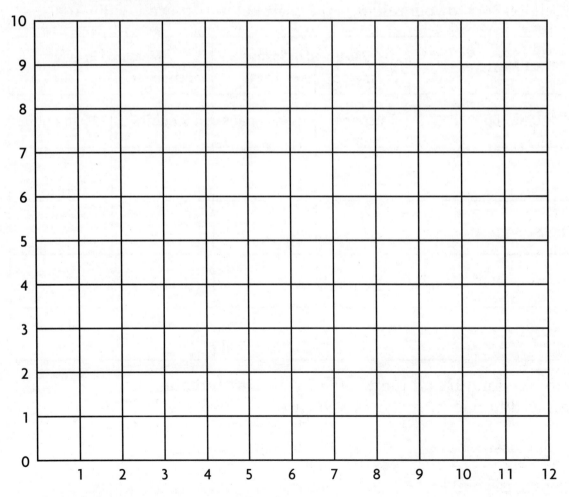

Harcourt Brace School Publishers

Flying Carpet Ride

Solve. You may use a calculator.

1. Jasmine took her flying carpet to Plume Island. She flew 4,638 miles north. Then she flew twice as many miles east. Finally, Jasmine flew south and reached Plume Island. She traveled 15,690 miles in all. How many miles was the last part of her trip?

_____ 1,776 mi _____

2. Jasmine's flying carpet not only flies—it also changes shape. The perimeter is always 32 feet. Jasmine needs the greatest area to take her new Plume Island friends for a ride. What shape will give her the greatest possible area? What are the lengths of the sides?

_____ square; 8 ft × 8 ft _____

3. Two Islanders offered to buy Jasmine's carpet. Tirian offered her $500. Miraz offered her $7.50 per square foot. If the perimeter of the square carpet equals 32 feet, who offered the most? How much more?

____ Tirian; $20 more than Miraz ____

4. Jasmine flew home by a more direct path. Her return flight was 5,555 miles shorter than her trip to Plume Island. How far was Jasmine's return flight? (Hint: See Problem 1.)

_____ 10,135 mi _____

5. Flying carpets give prizes if you travel more than 25,000 miles. Can Jasmine get a prize? How many miles did she fly? (Hint: See Problems 1 and 4.)

_____ yes; 25,825 mi _____

6. Write your own multistep problem about an adventure with a flying carpet. Show the solution upside down at the bottom of column 1.

_____ Check students' work. _____

_____

_____

_____

Answer:

Harcourt Brace School Publishers

Shapes in Motion

Here is your chance to practice flipping, turning, and
sliding figures to create a design.

Step 1 Read the numbers in the 4-by-4 grid.

Step 2 Replace the numbers with the matching symbols.

Step 3 Use two colors to create any design in the 4-by-4 grid.

1 = ◁
2 = ◹
3 = ◿
4 = ◸

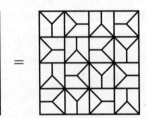 = 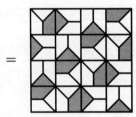 =

1	2	3	4
2	3	4	1
3	4	1	2
4	1	2	3

Complete using the steps above. **Designs will vary. Check students' work.**

1.

3	3	3	3
1	1	1	1
3	3	3	3
1	1	1	1

=

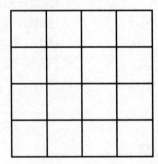

2.

1	3	3	1
4	2	4	2
3	1	1	3
1	3	3	1

=

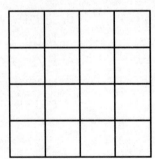

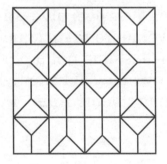

Use the puzzles above to help you create your own design. **Designs will vary. Check students' work.**

3.

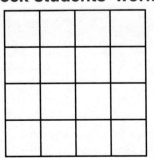

=

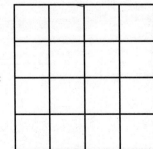

Harcourt Brace School Publishers

It's Hip to Be Square

Divide each square into the number of smaller squares
written beside it. Two examples are given. **Solutions may vary.**

Example 1

9 squares

1	2	3
4	5	6
7	8	9

Example 2

7 squares

1. 4 squares

| 1 | 2 |
| 3 | 4 |

2. 10 squares

1	2	5	6
3	4	7	8
9		10	

3. 12 squares

1	2	3 4
		5 6
7	8	9
10	11	12

4. 13 squares

1	2	5	6
3	4	7	8
9		10	11
		12	13

5. 16 squares

1		2
3	4 5	13	14
	6 7		
8 9	12	15	16
10 11			

6. 22 squares

1	2	3	4 5
			6 7
8	9	10 11	14
		12 13	
15	16	17	18
19	20	21	22

Harcourt Brace School Publishers

Snowflake Symmetry

Snowflakes are symmetrical ice crystals, exhibiting both line symmetry and point symmetry. You can experiment with symmetry by making your own snowflakes.

a. Start with a square piece of paper.	**b.** Fold the square in half.	**c.** Fold in half again.
d. Fold in half again, along the diagonal.	**e.** Cut out various polygons to make a design.	**f.** Open the paper and find a symmetrical snowflake pattern.

1. Use square pieces of paper to cut out five different snowflakes.

2. Test each snowflake. Mark a central point in the middle of a snowflake.

3. Place the snowflake on a sheet of paper. Trace around the snowflake. Shade in the holes of the snowflake.

4. Place a pencil on the central point. Rotate the snowflake.

   Do your snowflakes have point symmetry? ____**yes**____

Harcourt Brace School Publishers

Rorschach Inkblot Art

An inkblot is sometimes used in personality testing. The symmetrical image suggests different images to different people. You can make your own inkblot.

Follow these instructions to help you make two inkblots.

- Fold a piece of paper in half.

- Open it out flat.

- Place a few drops of ink inside. Then fold and press.

- Open your paper up and look at your inkblot.

Complete the inkblot survey. Ask three friends to participate. Record your results below. **Results will vary.**

INKBLOT SURVEY

Name	Inkblot 1	Upside Down	Inkblot 2	Upside Down
What I see				
What _____ sees				
What _____ sees				
What _____ sees				

Harcourt Brace School Publishers

Where in the World Is Terry Tessellation?

Tessellations can be found everywhere: from the elaborate castles and cathedrals of Europe to the brick walls and tile floors of your school.

Your mission is to seek out tessellations—at school, at home, and in books and magazines. Record in the chart the patterns you find and where you find them. **Answers will vary.**

Tessellation Pattern	Where Found
1.	brick wall outside the gym
2.	
3.	
4.	
5.	
6.	
7.	

Harcourt Brace School Publishers

Alphabet Exploration

1. Can you draw this shape 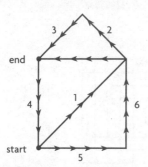 without lifting your pencil and without retracing any line? Give it a try below. **Possible answer.**

2. Now try the alphabet. In the space below, try writing each capital letter without lifting your pencil and without retracing any line.

3. Which letters were you not able to create? _____

Possible answer: A, E, F, H, I, J, K, T, X, Y

4. Write in the space below the capital letters of the alphabet that have line symmetry. Show the line of symmetry for each. **Possible answers:**

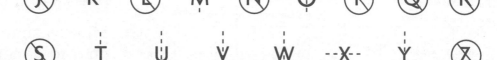

5. Write the letters of the alphabet that do not have line symmetry.

F, G, J, L, N, P, Q, R, S, Z

6. Use the grid to create your own artistic alphabet. See if you can make some symmetrical letters like those shown.

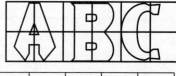

Harcourt Brace School Publishers

Artful Grids

Did you know that artists use grids to make two-dimensional sketches into three-dimensional sculptures? The most famous example is Mount Rushmore, where grids were created on the mountainside by hanging ropes.

You too can make a three-dimensional sculpture from a two-dimensional grid design. Here's how: **Check students' work.**

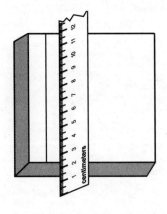 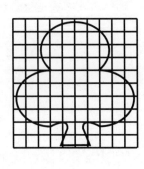 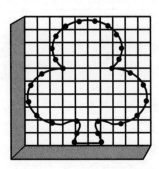 

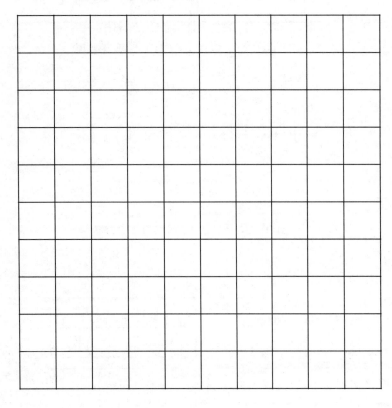

1. Roll modeling clay into a 10-cm x 10-cm square that is 1 centimeter thick. Place on a piece of paper.

2. Use a straightedge to press a grid onto the clay.

3. Make a simple design on grid paper.

4. Place your design on top of the clay. Use a paper clip to poke the outline of your design into the clay.

5. Move your design away and trim away extra clay.

Harcourt Brace School Publishers

Multiplication Bingo

Master basic multiplication facts with a friendly game of multiplication bingo. Play with several students. **Check students' answers as they play.**

To play:

- Have one player call out basic multiplication facts from 0×0 to 9×9.
- Look for the product of the basic fact on your bingo board. When you find a product, place a scrap of paper on that number.
- The first player to complete a row across, down, or diagonally says "Multiplication Bingo."

CARD A

32	25	18	36	0
6	56	20	81	48
63	49	FREE	27	28
24	15	35	40	72
42	21	56	16	30

CARD B

54	24	12	21	36
35	4	0	15	6
20	72	FREE	42	25
48	9	27	81	64
30	14	56	28	8

Harcourt Brace School Publishers

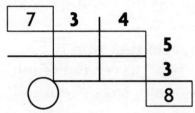

Name _____

Cross-Number Puzzles

You can use a cross-number puzzle to practice multiplication facts. Follow these steps to complete a cross-number puzzle for 7×8.

Step 1 Write 7 and 8 in the boxes as shown.

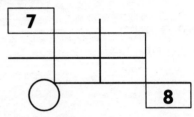

Step 2 Write addends for 7 across the top and addends for 8 down the right side.

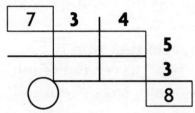

Step 3 Write partial products in the interior boxes.

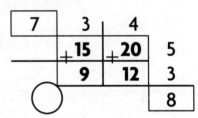

Step 4 Write the sum of the four partial products in the circle.

So, $7 \times 8 = 56$

Complete the cross-number puzzles to find the products.

1. $6 \times 9 =$

6	2	4	
+36	+12	+24	6
18	6	12	3
(54)	18+ 36		9

2. $5 \times 8 =$

5	2	3	
+25	+10	+15	5
15	6	9	3
(40)	16+ 24		8

3. $7 \times 4 =$

7	3	4	
+14	+6	+8	2
14	6	8	2
(28)	12+ 16		4

4. If you make a cross-number puzzle for 7×4 and use the following numbers, will you get the same final product of 28? __yes__

$7 \times 4 =$

7	2	5	
+7	+2	+5	1
21	6	15	3
(28)	8 + 20		4

Harcourt Brace School Publishers

Hand-y Multiplication

A handy method for multiplying with facts with 9s is
finger multiplication.

Use both hands with fingers spread apart.
Label the fingers consecutively from 1 to 10, as shown.

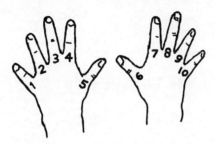

To multiply, bend the "multiplier finger." For the basic fact
3×9, you bend finger number 3, as shown below.

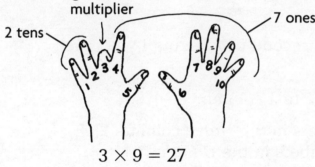

multiplier

2 tens

7 ones

$3 \times 9 = 27$

The fingers to the left of the multiplier give the tens in the
product. The fingers to the right of the multiplier give the
ones in the product.

Solve by using finger multiplication. Draw a picture of what each
hand looks like.

1. $7 \times 9 =$ __63__

6 tens   multiplier   3 ones

2. $5 \times 9 =$ __45__

4 tens   multiplier   5 ones

Harcourt Brace School Publishers

Doubling and Halving

One of the earliest methods of multiplying was accomplished through doubling and halving. This method can be traced to the early Egyptians.

Here is how to multiply 7×35:

Double		Halve	
7	$\times$	35	
14		17	← Half of 35 is $17\frac{1}{2}$; use only 17.
~~28~~		~~8~~	← Half of 17 is $8\frac{1}{2}$; use only 8.
~~56~~		~~4~~	
~~112~~		~~2~~	
224		1	

- Halve the numbers in the second column until you reach the number 1.

- Double the numbers in the first column.

- Cross out the even numbers in the *Halve* column: 2, 4, and 8. Then cross off numbers in the *Double* column that are opposite the crossed-off numbers.

- Add the numbers in the *Double* column that are not crossed out:
$7 + 14 + 224 = 245$

Multiply, using the doubling and halving method. Show your work.

1. $6 \times 42 =$

~~6~~	~~42~~
12	21
~~24~~	~~10~~
48	5
~~96~~	~~2~~
192	1

252 is the answer.

2. $3 \times 27 =$

3	27
6	13
~~12~~	~~6~~
24	3
48	1

81 is the answer.

3. $4 \times 51 =$

4	51
8	25
~~16~~	~~12~~
~~32~~	~~6~~
64	3
128	1

204 is the answer.

Harcourt Brace School Publishers

Comparison Shopping

To find the better buy, find the individual item price.

The music store offers CDs at $10.99 each or 5 for $44.95.
Which is the better deal?

- You can multiply the individual CD price by 5 to compare.
  $10.99 × 5 = $54.95 versus 5 for $44.95.

- Or you can divide the 5-pack price of $44.95 by 5 and compare.
  $44.95 ÷ 5 = $8.99 each versus $10.99 each.

The package deal for 5 CDs is the better buy.

Determine the better buy.

1. Fancy chocolate candies—
    14-piece box for $24.92 or
    each piece for $2.00?

    14-piece box

2. Batteries—
    2 for $1.57 or
    8 for $6.42?

    2 for $1.57

3. Eggs—
    $0.79 for 6 or
    $1.49 for 12?

    $1.49 for 12

4. Ice cream—
    1 half gallon for $1.89 or
    3 half gallons for $5.76?

    1 half gallon for $1.89

5. Coffee cups—
    1 for $0.89 or
    12 for $9.00?

    12 for $9.00

6. Butter—
    1 stick for $0.49 or
    4 sticks for $1.96?

    same price either way

7. Colored pencils—
    1 for $0.66 or
    6 for $4.10?

    1 for $0.66

8. Laundry detergent—
    64 oz for $2.99 or
    128 oz for $5.99?

    64 oz for $2.99

9. Spring water—
    1.5 liter for $1.69 or
    3.0 liter for $2.99?

    3.0 L for $2.99

10. Granola bars—
    4 for $2.96 or
    12 for $8.40?

    12 for $8.40

Harcourt Brace School Publishers

Napier's Rods

John Napier, a Scottish mathematician, lived about 400 years ago. He invented the series of multiplication rods shown below.

Guide ×	0	1	2	3	4	5	6	7	8	9
1	0/0	0/1	0/2	0/3	0/4	0/5	0/6	0/7	0/8	0/9
2	0/0	0/2	0/4	0/6	0/8	1/0	1/2	1/4	1/6	1/8
3	0/0	0/3	0/6	0/9	1/2	1/5	1/8	2/1	2/4	2/7
4	0/0	0/4	0/8	1/2	1/6	2/0	2/4	2/8	3/2	3/6
5	0/0	0/5	1/0	1/5	2/0	2/5	3/0	3/5	4/0	4/5
6	0/0	0/6	1/2	1/8	2/4	3/0	3/6	4/2	4/8	5/4
7	0/0	0/7	1/4	2/1	2/8	3/5	4/2	4/9	5/6	6/3
8	0/0	0/8	1/6	2/4	3/2	4/0	4/8	5/6	6/4	7/2
9	0/0	0/9	1/8	2/7	3/6	4/5	5/4	6/3	7/2	8/1

You can use Napier's rods to multiply 4×537.

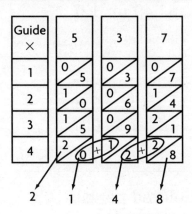

- Line up the guide rod and the rods for 5, 3, and 7.

- Look at the numbers in the fourth row. Start at the right, add the numbers as shown. Then write them as shown.

- The answer is 2,148.

Copy or cut out the rods above. Use the Napier's rods to find the products.

1. $6 \times 549 = $ __**3,294**__

2. $4 \times 375 = $ __**1,500**__

3. $3 \times 627 = $ __**1,881**__

4. $2 \times 125 = $ __**250**__

5. $7 \times 194 = $ __**1,358**__

6. $5 \times 431 = $ __**2,155**__

Harcourt Brace School Publishers

The Bigger, the Better

Players: 3 or more

Materials: Index cards numbered 1–9

Rules:

- One player draws six cards and pauses after each draw so that other players have time to decide where to write each digit.

- Players write the digits to make factors that give the greatest possible product. In every round, each player may throw out one digit.

- Once a player has written a digit, he or she cannot move the digit to another position.

- When the six cards have been drawn, players multiply to find their products. The player who has the greatest product wins the round.

Number
Thrown Out
↓

Round 1 ☐ ☐ ☐ ○
        X ☐ ☐
_____

Number
Thrown Out
↓

Round 2 ☐ ☐ ☐ ○
        X ☐ ☐
_____

Round 3 ☐ ☐ ☐ ○
        X ☐ ☐
_____

Round 4 ☐ ☐ ☐ ○
        X ☐ ☐
_____

Round 5 ☐ ☐ ☐ ○
        X ☐ ☐
_____

Round 6 ☐ ☐ ☐ ○
        X ☐ ☐
_____

Harcourt Brace School Publishers

The Powers That Be

You can shorten some large numbers by using **exponents** that are powers of ten. An exponent tells how many times to multiply a number by itself.

$10^0 = 1$

$10^1 = 10$

$10^2 = 10 \times 10 = 100$

$10^3 = 10 \times 10 \times 10 = 1,000$

As you can see, the exponent also tells how many zeros follow the number 1.

Many scientists round large numbers and use exponents.

One million equals 10^6. 18 million equals 18×10^6.

Draw a line to the matching number.

1. 32,000		89×10^5
2. 48,000,000		17×10^0
3. 560		9×10^6
4. 7,700		77×10^2
5. 8,900,000		32×10^3
6. 690,000		44×10^5
7. 9,000,000		16×10^7
8. 28,000		48×10^6
9. 17		98×10^6
10. 4,400,000		28×10^3
11. 160,000,000		56×10^1
12. 98,000,000		69×10^4

Harcourt Brace School Publishers

Probable-Products Game

Players: 3 or more

Materials: Calculator

Rules:

- One player writes a problem (for example, 84 × 36). He or she uses the calculator to find the product and keeps the product a secret.

- The other players estimate the product as closely as possible. Make no written computations. Write your estimate in your table.

- The player who wrote the problem tells the product.

- Points are given as follows:

  1 point if the greatest digit matches the exact answer

  2 points for the correct number of digits

  3 points for the closest estimate of the group

  4 points for an exact answer

Round	Problem	My Estimate	Exact Product	Points for the Round	Cumulative Points
example	84 × 36 = ?	3,200	3,024	1 + 2	3
1					
2					
3					
4					
5					
6					
7					
8					
9					
				Total	

Harcourt Brace School Publishers

Sport Triumphs

Pictographs are used to make visual comparisons of data.

This pictograph compares the number of completed passes by well-known National Football League (NFL) quarterbacks.

Quarterback	1994 Football Season
Steve Young	🏈🏈🏈🏈🏈🏈🏈 🏈🏈🏈🏈🏈🏈
Dan Marino	🏈🏈🏈🏈🏈🏈🏈🏈 🏈🏈🏈🏈🏈🏈🏈◀
Warren Moon	🏈🏈🏈🏈🏈🏈🏈🏈 🏈🏈🏈🏈🏈🏈🏈
Troy Aikman	🏈🏈🏈🏈🏈🏈 🏈🏈🏈🏈◀
Stan Humphries	🏈🏈🏈🏈🏈◀ 🏈🏈🏈🏈🏈

🏈 = 25 pass completions

1. Who had the most pass completions? _____ **Dan Marino**

2. Who had the fewest completions? _____ **Troy Aikman**

3. About how many pass completions did each quarterback throw?
   Possible answers are given.

   Steve Young ____ 325 ____   Troy Aikman ____ 233 ____

   Dan Marino ____ 387 ____   Stan Humphries ____ 263 ____

   Warren Moon ____ 375 ____

4. Use the following data on baseball home-run hitters to create your own pictograph. **Check students' graphs.**

Baseball Player	Lifetime Home Runs
Hank Aaron	755
Babe Ruth	714
Willie Mays	660
Frank Robinson	586
Reggie Jackson	563
Mickey Mantle	536

Harcourt Brace School Publishers

Name _____

Digit Detective

Complete the problem by finding the missing digits.

1.
```
      [7] 5
   ×   7 [5]
   [3]  7  5
   5, 2  5  0
   5, 6  2  5
```

2.
```
      3   2
   ×  4  [7]
   2  [2]  4
1,  2   8   0
1, [5]  0   4
```

3.
```
      5  [8]
   ×  3   3
      1   7   4
1,  [7]  4   0
1,  [9]  1   4
```

4.
```
      6  [4]
   × [2]  4
   2   5  [6]
1,  2  [8]  0
1,  5   3   6
```

5.
```
     [4]  7
   ×  5  [3]
      1  [4][1]
[2], [3]  5   0
 2,   4   9   1
```

6.
```
      5   4
   ×  3  [6]
   [3][2][4]
1,  6   2   0
1,  9   4   4
```

7.
```
      8  [3]
   × [6]  5
      4   1   5
   4,  9   8   0
   5,  3   9   5
```

8.
```
      7   3
   × [5]  4
   2  [9][2]
3,  6  [5]  0
3,  9  [4][2]
```

9.
```
        3  [5]
   ×   [5]  3
       1  [0]  5
 [1], [7]  5   0
  1,   8   5   5
```

10. Use the space below to create your own multiplication problems with missing digits. Ask a classmate to complete them. **Check students' problems.**

Harcourt Brace School Publishers

Doubling Tales

An ancient story tells of a clever traveling storyteller. He promised to entertain the king, and at a price that seemed unbeatable. For the first day the storyteller wanted only 1¢, and for each day after that the rate would double. The king thought about it briefly: 1¢ on day 1, 2¢ on day 2, and 4¢ on day 3. The king assumed that the price was reasonable.

How much will the storyteller charge the king on day 26?

Complete the table to find out. You may use a calculator.

Day	Price
1	1¢
2	2¢
3	4¢
4	8¢
5	16¢
6	32¢
7	64¢
8	$1.28
9	$2.56
10	$5.12
11	$10.24
12	$20.48
13	$40.96

Day	Price
14	$81.92
15	$163.84
16	$327.68
17	$655.36
18	$1,310.72
19	$2,621.44
20	$5,242.88
21	$10,485.76
22	$20,971.52
23	$41,943.04
24	$83,886.08
25	$167,772.16
26	$335,544.32

Do you think the storyteller charged a reasonable price? Explain.

Answers may vary.

_____

Harcourt Brace School Publishers

Cookie Coordinating

Joe and Melissa are organizing cookies to sell at a bake
sale. They are making equal groups of each kind of cookie.

Complete the chart.

Total Number ÷ Number of Plates = Number of Cookies
on Each Plate

	Kind of Cookie	Total Number	Number on Each Plate	Number of Plates
	Chocolate chip	96		12 $12 \times 8 = 96$ $96 \div 12 = 8$
1.	Oatmeal	42		14 $14 \times 3 = 42$ $42 \div 14 = 3$
2.	Peanut butter	91		13 $13 \times 7 = 91$ $91 \div 13 = 7$
3.	Butterscotch	76		19 $19 \times 4 = 76$ $76 \div 19 = 4$
4.	Sugar	90		18 $18 \times 5 = 90$ $90 \div 18 = 5$
5.	Ginger	36		12 $12 \times 3 = 36$ $36 \div 12 = 3$

6. How many plates in all did Joe and Melissa use? _____ **88 plates**

Harcourt Brace School Publishers

Number Riddles

To solve the riddles on this page, you will need to know the name for each part of a division problem. Use the example at the right as a reminder.

quotient —— 9 r1 —— remainder
divisor — 4)‾3‾7 —— dividend

1. My divisor is 5.
   I am greater than 4 × 5.
   I am less than 5 × 5.
   My remainder is 1.

   What dividend am I? __21__

2. My divisor is 9.
   I am greater than 7 × 9.
   I am less than 8 × 9.
   My remainder is 7.

   What dividend am I? __70__

3. My divisor is 8.
   I am less than 30.
   I am greater than 3 × 8.
   My remainder is 5.

   What dividend am I? __29__

4. My divisor is 6.
   I am less than 60.
   I am greater than 8 × 6.
   I have no remainder.

   What dividend am I? __54__

5. My dividend is 50.
   My divisor is an odd number.
   My remainder is 1.

   What divisor am I? __7__

6. My dividend is 8 times larger than my divisor.
   I am an even number less than 15.

   What quotient am I? __8__

7. My remainder is 8.
   My dividend is 80.
   I am a 1-digit number.

   What divisor am I? __9__

8. My dividend is 24.
   My divisor is 2 more than my quotient.
   I have no remainder.

   What divisor am I? __6__

Complete these equations.

9. (__5__ × __5__) + 2 = 27

10. (__3__ × __7__) + 5 = 26 **or 7 × 3**

11. (__7__ × __7__) + 3 = 52

12. (__5__ × __7__) + 1 = 36 **or 7 × 5**

13. Write your own number riddle below.

   __Check students' work.__ _____

   _____

Harcourt Brace School Publishers

Remainders Game

Number of players: 2, 3, or 4

Materials: game board
markers (24 small pieces of paper)
number cube with the numbers 3, 4, 5, 6, 7, and 8

Rules:

- Take turns placing a marker on one of the numbers on the board and rolling the number cube. Divide the numbers. For example, if you choose 92 on the board and roll a 3 on the number cube, you then write the problem $92 \div 3 = 30$ r2.

- Your score is equal to your remainder.

- After all the numbers on the board have been covered with markers, find the sum of your remainder scores. The winner is the player who has the greatest total score.

29	56	35	92	17	53
71	89	47	62	59	40
49	74	30	25	93	57
80	13	65	72	34	21

Harcourt Brace School Publishers

Break the Code

In the division problems below, each letter stands for a digit. The same letter stands for the same digit in all of the problems.

The table shows that H = 2 and T = 8. Use the division problems to find out what each of the other letters stands for.

0	1	2	3	4	5	6	7	8	9
A	L	H	R	D	E	I	F	T	W

Once you have broken the code, use the letters and digits to answer the riddle at the bottom of this page.

1.
```
       DD    44
   H)TT    2)88
    -8      -8
    08      08
   - 8     - 8
     0       0
```

2.
```
       LH    12
   D)DT    4)48
    -4      -4
    08      08
   - 8     - 8
     0       0
```

3.
```
        T     8
   I)DT    6)48
   -48     -48
     0       0
```

4.
```
       HT    28
   H)EI    2)56
    -4      -4
    16      16
   -16     -16
     0       0
```

5.
```
        T     8
   D)RH    4)32
   -32     -32
     0       0
```

6.
```
       LH    12
   E)IA    5)60
    -5      -5
    10      10
   -10     -10
     0       0
```

7.
```
      I rL    6 r1
   F)DR     7)43
    -42     -42
      1       1
```

8.
```
      HH rH    22 r2
   D)WA      4)90
    -8       -8
    10       10
   - 8      - 8
     2        2
```

HOW DID THE RIVER HURT ITSELF?

Code Letter	I	T		H	A	D		A		W	A	T	E	R	F	A	L	L
Digit	6	8		2	0	4		0		9	0	8	5	3	7	0	1	1

Harcourt Brace School Publishers

Grouping Possibilities

Complete each table by finding
different ways to divide a large
number into smaller groups while
always having the same remainder.

For example, $2\overline{)65}$ $\overset{32\,r1}{}$ works in table 1.

But $3\overline{)65}$ $\overset{21\,r2}{}$ does not work.

1.

Total	Number of Groups (less than 10)	Number in Each Group	Remainder
65	2	32	1
65	4	16	1
65	8	8	1

2.

Total	Number of Groups (less than 10)	Number in Each Group	Remainder
74	3	24	2
74	4	18	2
74	6	12	2
74	8	9	2
74	9	8	2

3.

Total	Number of Groups (less than 10)	Number in Each Group	Remainder
111	2	54	3
111	3	36	3
111	4	27	3
111	6	18	3
111	9	12	3

Harcourt Brace School Publishers

Digit Discovery

Write the missing digits.

1.
```
      [1] 6
  4 ) 6  4
    - 4
    [2][4]
    - 2  4
         0
```

2.
```
    2 [3] r2
  3 ) 7  1
    -[6]
     1 [1]
     -  9
        2
```

3.
```
    1 [4] r1
  5 ) 7  1
    - 5
     2  1
    -[2][0]
        1
```

4.
```
    [2] 5  1 r2
  3 ) 7  5  5
    - 6
    [1][5]
    - 1  5
        0  5
       -   [3]
           2
```

5.
```
    1 [3][6] r5
  6 )[8] 2  1
    - 6
     2 [2]
    - 1  8
        4 [1]
       - 3  6
           5
```

6.
```
      2 [4] r[3]
 [5] ) 1  2  3
     - 1  0
      [2] 3
      - 2  0
          [3]
```

7.
```
      2  7 r1
  3 )[8][2]
    -[6]
     [2][2]
    -[2][1]
           1
```

8.
```
      1  3  3
  7 )[9][3][1]
    -[7]
     [2][3]
    -[2][1]
        [2][1]
       -[2][1]
            0
```

9.
```
        4  7 r3
  6 )[2][8][5]
    -[2][4]
       [4][5]
      -[4][2]
          [3]
```

Harcourt Brace School Publishers

The Smaller Quotient Wins!

Play with a partner.

Getting Ready to Play:

- Trace and cut out the number pieces and game boards.
- Place the number pieces into a paper bag.

To Play:

- Take turns choosing a number piece and placing it in one of the 4 spaces on the game board.
- After each player has filled a game board, solve the division problem on a piece of scratch paper.
- Check each other's quotient by using multiplication.
- The player with the smaller quotient wins.
- Put the number pieces back and play again.

Number Pieces

0	1	2	3	4	5	6	7	8	9
0	1	2	3	4	5	6	7	8	9

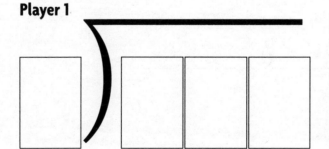

Game Board

Player 1

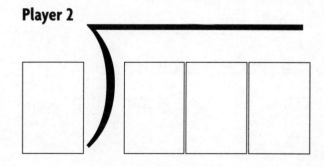

Game Board

Player 2

Harcourt Brace School Publishers

Riddle-jam

Riddle: What do geese do in a traffic jam?

Find each quotient. Then write the quotients in order from least to greatest at the bottom of the page. Write the matching letter below each quotient.

1. $450 \div 5 =$ __90__   Y   2. $270 \div 9 =$ __30__   T

3. $3,600 \div 9 =$ __400__   O   4. $42,000 \div 7 =$ __6,000__   L

5. $2,100 \div 7 =$ __300__   H   6. $7,200 \div 8 =$ __900__   K

7. $36,000 \div 9 =$ __4,000__   A   8. $280 \div 7 =$ __40__   H

9. $3,500 \div 7 =$ __500__   N   10. $240 \div 4 =$ __60__   E

11. $56,000 \div 7 =$ __8,000__   T   12. $49,000 \div 7 =$ __7,000__   O

Riddle Answer:

__30__ __40__ __60__ __90__   __300__ __400__ __500__ __900__
  T   H   E   Y   H   O   N   K

4,000   6,000 7,000 8,000
  A   L   O   T   !

Harcourt Brace School Publishers

Name _____

Name _____

Super Checker!

Solve each division problem. Then complete the number sentence
that can be used to check the answer. Draw a line from the
division problem to the related number sentence.

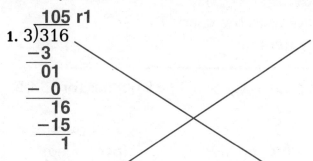

```
      105 r1
1. 3)316
     −3
      01
    − 0
      16
    −15
      1
```

```
      160
2. 5)800
     −5
      30
    −30
      00
    − 0
      0
```

```
      207 r3
3. 4)831
     −8
      03
    − 0
      31
    −28
      3
```

```
      309 r1
4. 2)619
     −6
      01
    − 0
      19
    −18
      1
```

```
      120 r2
5. 7)842
     −7
      14
    −14
      02
    − 0
      2
```

A.   (___5___ × 160) = ___800___

B.   (___3___ × 105) + 1 = ___316___

C.   (___2___ × 309) + 1 = ___619___

D.   (___7___ × 120) + 2 = ___842___

E.   (___4___ × 207) + 3 = ___831___

Harcourt Brace School Publishers

More for Your Money

Some items are sold in different quantities, or in packages of different sizes. The unit price is the price for one unit of each item, such as the price per pound or the price per item.

Find the unit price for each of the grocery items in the chart. Then circle the lowest unit price for each grocery item.

Oranges	1 pound for $0.89	2 pounds for $1.70	5 pounds for $3.25
	Unit price (per pound)	Unit price (per pound)	Unit price (per pound)
	$0.89	$0.85	$0.65
Bagels	1 for $0.39	3 for $1.17	6 for $1.98
	Unit price (per bagel)	Unit price (per bagel)	Unit price (per bagel)
	$0.39	$0.39	$0.33
Cream Cheese	2 ounces for $0.46	4 ounces for $0.76	8 ounces for $1.12
	Unit price (per ounce)	Unit price (per ounce)	Unit price (per ounce)
	$0.23	$0.19	$0.14
Juice	1 quart for $0.79	2 quarts for $1.40	4 quarts for $2.96
	Unit price (per quart)	Unit price (per quart)	Unit price (per quart)
	$0.79	$0.70	$0.74
Cereal	6 ounces for $1.02	8 ounces for $1.60	9 ounces for $1.62
	Unit price (per ounce)	Unit price (per ounce)	Unit price (per ounce)
	$0.17	$0.20	$0.18

Harcourt Brace School Publishers

Shipping Basketballs

The Best Basketball Factory ships basketballs to sporting goods stores. The factory can ship basketballs in cartons of different sizes that hold either 1, 2, 4, or 8 basketballs.

1. Complete the chart to show 6 different ways that the Best Basketball Factory can ship 30 basketballs.
Answers will vary. Possible answers are given.

Carton for 1	Carton for 2	Carton for 4	Carton for 8	Total Number of Basketballs
2		7		30
	1	1	3	30
	1	3	2	30
	3	6		30
14			2	30
2		5	1	30

The factory saves money when it ships basketballs in the fewest number of cartons possible.

2. What is the fewest number of boxes that the factory can use to ship 30 basketballs?

_____ **5 cartons** _____

3. Complete the chart below to show how the factory can use the fewest number of cartons to ship the different numbers of basketballs.

Carton for 1	Carton for 2	Carton for 4	Carton for 8	Total Number of Basketballs
1	1	1	1	15
1	1	1	3	31
1	1	1	7	63
	1		15	122
1	1		31	251
		1	37	300

Harcourt Brace School Publishers

Diagram Division

Complete the division number sentence for each of the illustrations.

1.   Cookies

$98 \div 4 =$ __24__ r __2__

2.   Eggs

__77__ $\div$ __6__ $= 12\ r5$

3.   Marbles

$145 \div 3 =$ __48__ r __1__

4.   Crayons

__182__ $\div$ __5__ $= 36\ r2$

5.   Pennies in Piñatas

__\$9.87__ $\div$ __3__ $= \$3.29$

Harcourt Brace School Publishers

Find the Missing Scores

Mr. Murphy gave a math quiz to his students each day for
a week. The highest possible score was 12 points.

A group of 4 students kept a record of their scores for the week.

1. Complete the chart by filling in the missing numbers.

	Mon	Tue	Wed	Thu	Fri	Average score for each student
Hank	8 pts	9 pts	9 pts	12 pts	12 pts	10 pts
Jim	6 pts	9 pts	8 pts	9 pts	8 pts	8 pts
Sarah	5 pts	6 pts	7 pts	8 pts	9 pts	7 pts
Corina	9 pts	12 pts	12 pts	11 pts	11 pts	11 pts
Average score on each quiz	7 pts	9 pts	9 pts	10 pts	10 pts	9 pts

2. Which student had the highest average score?

_____ Corina _____

3. On which days was the average score for the 4 students
the highest?

_____ Thursday and Friday _____

4. What is the difference between Corina's average score
and the lowest average score?

_____ 4 pts _____

5. What does the number in the box at the lower right-
hand corner of the chart represent?

Possible answers: the average of the students' daily average

scores; the average of each students' weekly average score.

Harcourt Brace School Publishers

STRETCH YOUR THINKING   E119

What's for Lunch?

Joe's Lunch Bar					
Hot dog	$1.09	Juice, small	$0.39	Cookie	$0.50
Hamburger	$1.59	Juice, medium	$0.59	Brownie	$0.75
Slice of pizza	$1.25	Juice, large	$0.69	Ice cream bar	$1.25

Lunch Special $2.19
Hamburger, medium juice, cookie

1. Lucas bought a hot dog, a large juice, and an ice cream bar. How much money did he spend on lunch?

$3.03

2. Mr. Torres bought 4 lunch specials for his family. How much money did he spend?

$8.76

3. Tom bought 2 hamburgers and a medium juice. What was his change from a $5 bill?

$1.23

4. How much more does a hot dog, small juice, and a brownie cost than the lunch special?

$0.04

5. In one week, the shop sold 246 hot dogs. The shop is open 6 days a week. What was the average number of hot dogs sold each day?

41 hot dogs

6. On Monday, the cook made 6 whole pizzas. He cut each pizza into 8 slices. At the end of the day, there were 3 slices left over. How many slices of pizza did the shop sell that day?

45 slices

7. During one week, the shop sold 272 slices of pizza. If each whole pizza is cut into 8 slices, how many whole pizzas did the shop sell during the week?

34 pizzas

8. The shop sold 4 dozen brownies on Tuesday. How much money did the shop take in from brownie sales?

$36.00

Harcourt Brace School Publishers

A Fraction of a Message

Decode the message. Find the fraction in the boxes below that
represents each letter on the number line. Write the letter of
that fraction in the message boxes.

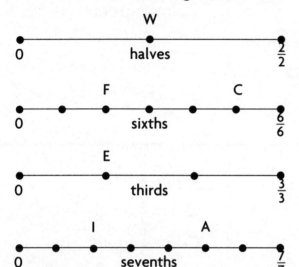

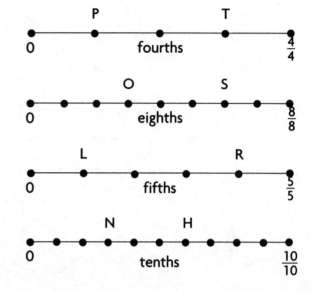

The message:

$\frac{5}{7}$
A

$\frac{2}{6}$	$\frac{4}{5}$	$\frac{5}{7}$	$\frac{5}{6}$	$\frac{3}{4}$	$\frac{2}{7}$	$\frac{3}{8}$	$\frac{3}{10}$
F	R	A	C	T	I	O	N

$\frac{2}{7}$	$\frac{6}{8}$
I	S

$\frac{5}{7}$
A

$\frac{1}{4}$	$\frac{5}{7}$	$\frac{4}{5}$	$\frac{3}{4}$
P	A	R	T

$\frac{3}{8}$	$\frac{2}{6}$
O	F

$\frac{5}{7}$
A

$\frac{1}{2}$	$\frac{6}{10}$	$\frac{3}{8}$	$\frac{1}{5}$	$\frac{1}{3}$
W	H	O	L	E

Make up your own coded message or riddle using the
number lines above. Add extra letters if you need them.

Answers will vary.
_____

_____

_____

_____

Harcourt Brace School Publishers

Colorful Fractions

Follow the directions. Color each part. **Check students' answers.**

1.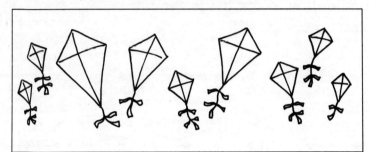

Color $\frac{1}{3}$ red.

Color $\frac{2}{3}$ green.

2.

Color $\frac{2}{5}$ red.

Color $\frac{2}{5}$ blue.

Color $\frac{1}{5}$ green.

3.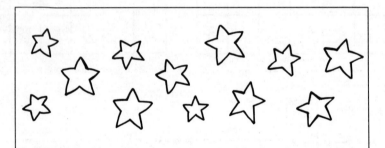

Color $\frac{1}{4}$ blue.

Color $\frac{2}{4}$ red.

Color $\frac{1}{4}$ green.

4.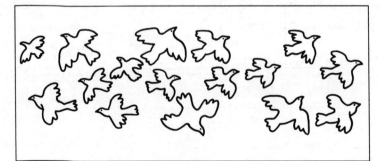

Color $\frac{1}{8}$ blue.

Color $\frac{2}{8}$ red.

Color $\frac{4}{8}$ green.

Color $\frac{1}{8}$ yellow.

Harcourt Brace School Publishers

Equivalent Fraction Bingo!

Use your math skills with equivalent fractions to play bingo!

Materials:

2 number cubes, counters to cover gameboard,
fraction bars

To Play:

- The object of the game is to cover a row—horizontally, vertically, or diagonally—with counters.

- Roll a number cube two times. Using one number as the numerator and one number as the denominator, write a fraction less than or equal to one. Place a counter on a fraction that is equivalent to the one you made.

  For example, if you roll a 6 and a 4, the fraction you write is $\frac{4}{6}$. Look for an equivalent fraction such as $\frac{2}{3}$. Cover the space marked $\frac{2}{3}$ on the gameboard. (Use the fraction strips to help find equivalent fractions.)

Gameboard

$\frac{1}{4}$	$\frac{1}{5}$	$\frac{6}{6}$	$\frac{3}{5}$	$\frac{1}{2}$
1	$\frac{2}{3}$	$\frac{5}{6}$	$\frac{4}{5}$	$\frac{1}{4}$
$\frac{3}{4}$	$\frac{1}{3}$	FREE	$\frac{1}{2}$	1
$\frac{3}{5}$	1	$\frac{1}{6}$	$\frac{1}{4}$	$\frac{2}{5}$
$\frac{1}{2}$	$\frac{3}{4}$	$\frac{2}{3}$	1	$\frac{1}{3}$

Harcourt Brace School Publishers

Name _____

Estimating Fractional Parts

You can estimate the part of a whole that is shaded by
thinking about benchmark fractions.

Example About what part of this rectangle is shaded?
Is $\frac{1}{3}$ or $\frac{1}{2}$ the better estimate?

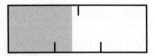

$\frac{1}{3}$ shaded would look like this. $\frac{1}{2}$ shaded would look like this.

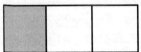   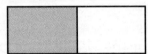

The part shaded is closer to $\frac{1}{2}$ than to $\frac{1}{3}$. So, $\frac{1}{2}$ is the better estimate.

What amount of the figure is shaded? Circle the fraction that is
the closer estimate.

1.

$\left(\frac{7}{8}\right)$ or $\frac{3}{4}$

2.

$\left(\frac{2}{3}\right)$ or $\frac{5}{6}$

3.

$\frac{1}{3}$ or $\left(\frac{1}{4}\right)$

4.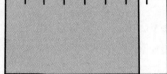

$\frac{4}{6}$ or $\left(\frac{5}{12}\right)$

5.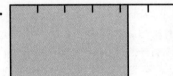

$\frac{2}{3}$ or $\left(\frac{5}{6}\right)$

6.

$\frac{2}{3}$ or $\left(\frac{11}{12}\right)$

7.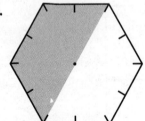

$\frac{3}{4}$ or $\left(\frac{5}{8}\right)$

8.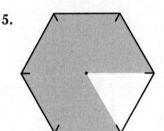

$\left(\frac{1}{4}\right)$ or $\frac{3}{8}$

9.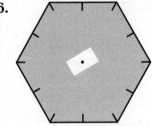

$\frac{1}{4}$ or $\left(\frac{1}{3}\right)$

Harcourt Brace School Publishers

E124 STRETCH YOUR THINKING

Language Exploration

Use a dictionary to help you complete this page.

A **centi**meter is one hundredth of a meter.

1. How many centimeters are in a meter? ____ **100 centimeters** ____

2. List several words that contain the root word "cent" and give their meanings. **Possible answers: century—a group or series of 100 like things; centavo—means "hundredth" and is a Spanish coin; percent—one part of one hundred**

A **tri**angle has three angles.

3. How many sides has a triangle? ____ **3 sides** ____

4. List several words that begin with "tri" and give their meanings.

Possible answers: triathlon—a contest of 3 events: bicycling, running, and swimming; Triassac—the earliest of 3 parts of time used to measure geology; triad—a musical chord of 3 tones

A **milli**liter is one thousandth of a liter.

5. How many milliliters are in a liter? ____ **1,000 mL** ____

6. List several words that begin with "mill" and give their meanings.

Possible answers: millipede—a small creature with lots of feet; millionaire—a person whose wealth is a million or more dollars; millennium—a period of 1,000 years

7. What does "bicycle" mean? ____ **a vehicle with two wheels** ____

8. Name other common words that begin with "bi," where "bi" means "two." **Possible answers: bicep—a muscle that has two heads connecting to the bone; bifocal—eyeglasses with two-part lenses; bilingual—able to speak two languages**

Harcourt Brace School Publishers

Name _____

A Mixed-Number Challenge

Work together with a partner to write a number that tells how much is shaded.

1.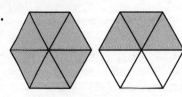

_____ $1\frac{3}{6}$, or $1\frac{1}{2}$ _____

2.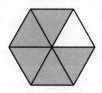

_____ $2\frac{1}{6}$ _____

Write a mixed number for each of the following figures. The figure at the right stands for 1.

3.

_____ $1\frac{1}{6}$ _____

4.

_____ $2\frac{2}{6}$, or $2\frac{1}{3}$ _____

5.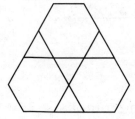

_____ $3\frac{4}{6}$, or $3\frac{2}{3}$ _____

6.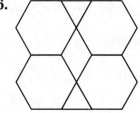

_____ $4\frac{4}{6}$, or $4\frac{2}{3}$ _____

7.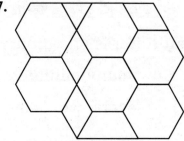

_____ $7\frac{4}{6}$, or $7\frac{2}{3}$ _____

Shade parts of the following figures. Have a partner write a mixed number that tells how much is shaded. **Answers will vary.**

8.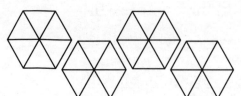

_____

9.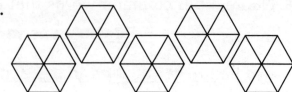

_____

Harcourt Brace School Publishers

Name _____

Amazing Maze

Find the path from the beginning to the end of the maze. Start with $\frac{1}{12}$ and add each fraction along your path. Your goal is to end up at the finish with $6\frac{10}{12}$.

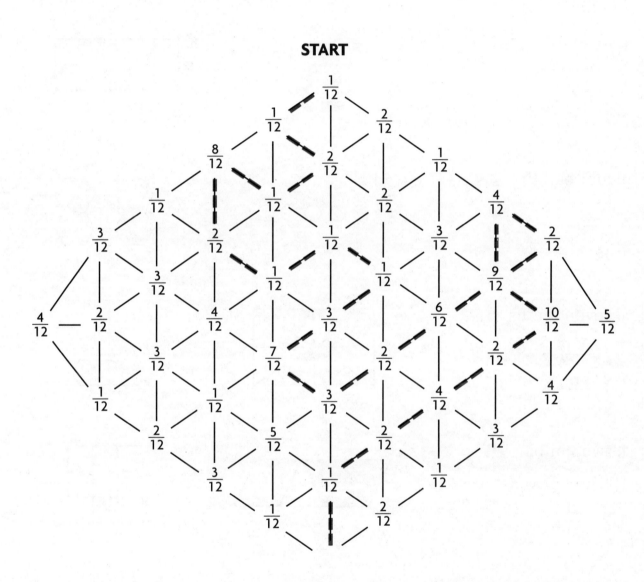

Harcourt Brace School Publishers

Name That Fraction

Fractions can be described with numbers, words, or pictures.

Number	Word	Picture
$\frac{3}{4}$	three fourths	

Match the fractions with the words or pictures that they best describe.

1. one half ___i___

2. $\frac{4}{7}$ ___d___

3. four eighths ___e___

4. $\frac{5}{12}$ ___j___

5. seven tenths ___b___

6. $\frac{3}{7}$ ___c___

7. two ninths ___h___

8. $\frac{3}{4}$ ___a___

9. five sixths ___f___

10. $\frac{4}{6}$ ___g___

a.

b.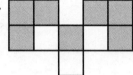

c.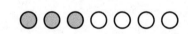

d.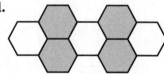

e.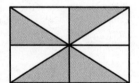

f.

g.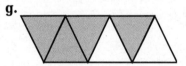

h.

i.

j.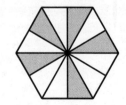

Harcourt Brace School Publishers

Name _____

What's Left?

Color each picture as directed. Colors do not overlap.
When you are finished coloring, answer each question. **Check students' coloring.**

1. Color $\frac{1}{3}$ of the cake red.

   Color $\frac{1}{3}$ of the cake brown.

   How much of the cake is not

   colored? ____$\frac{1}{3}$____

   How much of the cake is

   colored? ____$\frac{2}{3}$____

2. Color $\frac{6}{15}$ of the figure brown.

   Color $\frac{6}{15}$ of the figure orange.

   What fraction of the figure is

   not colored? ____$\frac{3}{15}$____

   What fraction of the figure is

   colored? ____$\frac{12}{15}$____

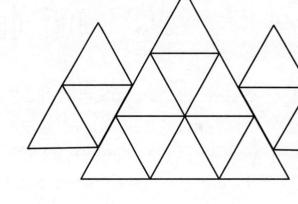

3. Color $\frac{8}{18}$ of the flag red.

   Color $\frac{2}{18}$ of the flag green.

   Color $\frac{2}{18}$ of the flag blue.

   Color $\frac{6}{18}$ of the flag orange.

   What fraction of the flag is not

   colored? ____$\frac{0}{18}$____

   What fraction of the flag is

   colored? ____$\frac{18}{18}$____

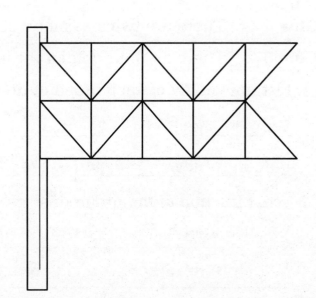

Harcourt Brace School Publishers

What Breed Is Each Dog?

There are 48 dogs at the dog show.

Clue 1	Every dog is a specific breed.
Clue 2	The different breeds of dogs are: German shepherds, cairn terriers, poodles, golden retrievers, and Labradors.
Clue 3	Half of the dogs are German shepherds.
Clue 4	There are an equal number of cairn terriers and poodles.
Clue 5	There are twice as many cairn terriers as Labradors.
Clue 6	There are four golden retrievers.

1. List how many of each breed of dog there are.

   <u>**German shepherds = 24, cairn terriers = 8, poodles = 8,**</u>

   <u>**golden retrievers = 4, and Labradors = 4**</u>

2. What fraction of the group does each breed of dog represent?

   German shepherds = $\frac{24}{48}$, cairn terriers = $\frac{8}{48}$, poodles = $\frac{8}{48}$,

   golden retrievers = $\frac{4}{48}$, and Labradors = $\frac{4}{48}$

Harcourt Brace School Publishers

Name _____

LESSON
21.4

All Mixed Up!

Draw a line to connect the problem with the correct sum.

s. $5\frac{1}{8} + 3\frac{1}{8} = ?$ • $7\frac{3}{10}$

E. $6\frac{1}{3} + 5\frac{1}{3} = ?$ • 9

E. $4\frac{1}{2} + 4\frac{1}{2} = ?$ • $13\frac{5}{8}$

N. $4\frac{2}{5} + 3\frac{1}{5} = ?$ • $11\frac{2}{12}$

V. $6\frac{3}{8} + 7\frac{2}{8} = ?$ • $14\frac{1}{4}$

T. $10\frac{3}{4} + 3\frac{2}{4} = ?$ • $8\frac{2}{8}$

I. $8\frac{3}{7} + 2\frac{2}{7} = ?$ • $18\frac{7}{9}$

A. $7\frac{1}{6} + 4\frac{1}{6} = ?$ • $7\frac{3}{5}$

E. $5\frac{2}{10} + 2\frac{1}{10} = ?$ • $8\frac{2}{4}$

N. $10\frac{1}{12} + 1\frac{1}{12} = ?$ • $11\frac{2}{3}$

E. $6\frac{1}{4} + 2\frac{1}{4} = ?$ • $11\frac{2}{6}$

N. $10\frac{2}{9} + 8\frac{5}{9} = ?$ • $10\frac{5}{7}$

To solve the riddle, match the letters above with the sums below the boxes.

Riddle: Why was six afraid of seven?

Answer: because $\boxed{S}\ \boxed{E}\ \boxed{V}\ \boxed{E}\ \boxed{N}$ $\boxed{A}\ \boxed{T}\ \boxed{E}$ (8) $\boxed{N}\ \boxed{I}\ \boxed{N}\ \boxed{E}$

$8\frac{2}{8}$ $8\frac{2}{4}$ $13\frac{5}{8}$ $7\frac{3}{10}$ $18\frac{7}{9}$ $11\frac{2}{6}$ $14\frac{1}{4}$ $11\frac{2}{3}$ $11\frac{2}{12}$ $10\frac{5}{7}$ $7\frac{3}{5}$ 9

Harcourt Brace School Publishers

STRETCH YOUR THINKING   E131

Shady Business!

Below each picture write the mixed number it represents. Then find each
difference. Draw a picture to show the answer.

1.

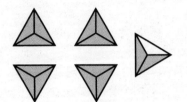

$$4\frac{2}{3} \qquad - \qquad 2\frac{1}{3} \qquad = \qquad 2\frac{1}{3}$$

2.

$$4\frac{4}{6} \qquad - \qquad 1\frac{2}{6} \qquad = \qquad 3\frac{2}{6}$$

3.

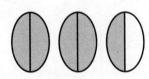

$$2\frac{1}{2} \qquad - \qquad 1\frac{1}{2} \qquad = \qquad 1$$

4.

 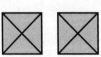 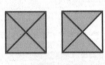

$$4\frac{3}{4} \qquad - \qquad 2\frac{1}{4} \qquad = \qquad 2\frac{2}{4}$$

Harcourt Brace School Publishers

Riddlegram!

Answer this riddle. Write the letter that matches each fraction or decimal.
You will use some models several times.

Riddle: Why do you measure snakes in inches?

$\underset{0.7}{\underline{\text{B}}}$ $\underset{\frac{35}{100}}{\underline{\text{E}}}$ $\underset{0.5}{\underline{\text{C}}}$ $\underset{0.52}{\underline{\text{A}}}$ $\underset{\frac{1}{10}}{\underline{\text{U}}}$ $\underset{\frac{15}{100}}{\underline{\text{S}}}$ $\underset{0.35}{\underline{\text{E}}}$ $\underset{0.2}{\underline{\text{T}}}$ $\underset{\frac{49}{100}}{\underline{\text{H}}}$ $\underset{\frac{35}{100}}{\underline{\text{E}}}$ $\underset{0.9}{\underline{\text{Y}}}$

$\underset{0.49}{\underline{\text{H}}}$ $\underset{\frac{52}{100}}{\underline{\text{A}}}$ $\underset{0.12}{\underline{\text{V}}}$ $\underset{\frac{35}{100}}{\underline{\text{E}}}$ $\underset{0.3}{\underline{\text{N}}}$ $\underset{\frac{8}{10}}{\underline{\text{O}}}$ $\underset{\frac{6}{10}}{\underline{\text{F}}}$ $\underset{0.35}{\underline{\text{E}}}$ $\underset{0.35}{\underline{\text{E}}}$ $\underset{\frac{2}{10}}{\underline{\text{T}}}$!

T
C
S
Y

H
N
A
O

V
B
U
E

F

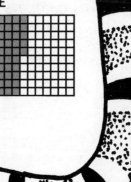

Harcourt Brace School Publishers

Add Them Up!

Each circle below is divided into tenths. Use different colored pencils to show two decimal numbers that equal one whole when added together. Complete the number sentence below each circle.

For Exercises 1–8, check students' drawings and number sentences. Answers will vary.

1.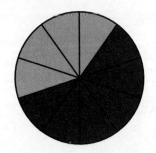

2.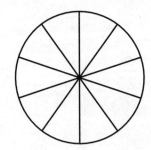

3.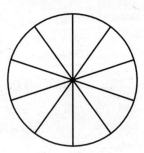

$0.4 + 0.6 = 1.0$

_____ + _____ = 1.0

_____ + _____ = 1.0

For each circle below, show 3 decimal numbers that equal one whole when added together. Complete the number sentence below each circle.

4.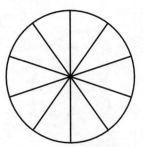

5.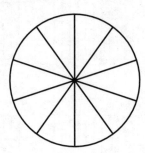

_____ + _____ + _____ = 1.0

_____ + _____ + _____ = 1.0

Each square below is divided into hundredths. Use different colored pencils to show two decimal numbers that equal one whole when added together. Complete the number sentence below each square.

6.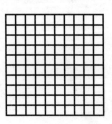

7.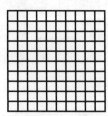

8.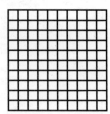

_____ + _____ = 1.0

_____ + _____ = 1.0

_____ + _____ = 1.0

Harcourt Brace School Publishers

Designing with Decimals

Shade in the decimal amount in each model.

1.

0.2

2.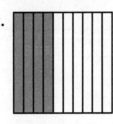

0.4

3.

0.8

4.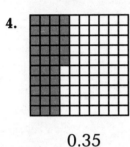

0.35

5.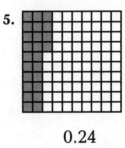

0.24

6.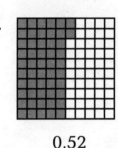

0.52

Complete. You may want to look at the shaded models above.

7. 2 tenths = __20__ hundredths

8. __4__ tenths = 40 hundredths

9. 35 hundredths = __3__ tenths and 5 hundredths

10. 2 tenths and 4 hundredths = __24__ hundredths

Use colored pencils to make a design or picture on the grid. Color in the decimal part indicated for each color. **Check students' drawings.**

Red = 0.25

Yellow = 0.30

Blue = 0.15

Black = 0.10

Green = 0.20

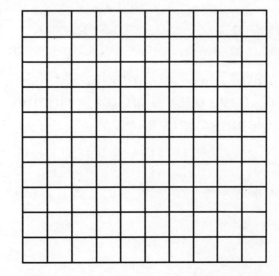

Harcourt Brace School Publishers

Missing Decimal Mystery

Write the numbers that are missing from each number line below.

1.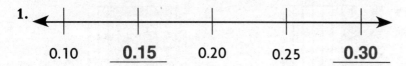

0.10   **0.15**   0.20   0.25   **0.30**

2.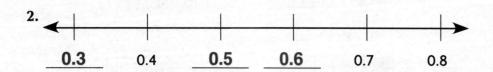

0.3   0.4   **0.5**   **0.6**   0.7   0.8

3.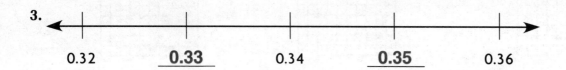

0.32   **0.33**   0.34   **0.35**   0.36

4.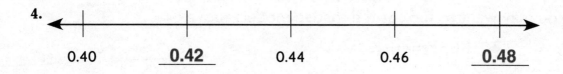

0.40   **0.42**   0.44   0.46   **0.48**

5.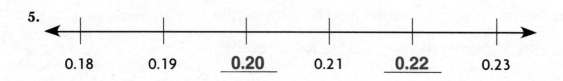

0.18   0.19   **0.20**   0.21   **0.22**   0.23

6.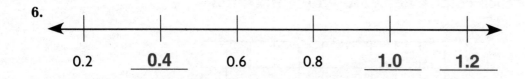

0.2   **0.4**   0.6   0.8   **1.0**   **1.2**

7. Make your own number line. Include the following
   numbers: 0.01, 0.12, 0.03, 0.09, 0.08, 0.15. **Number lines
   may vary. A possible answer is shown.**

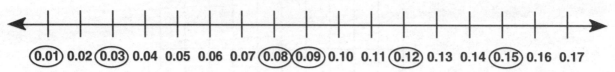

(0.01) 0.02 (0.03) 0.04 0.05 0.06 0.07 (0.08)(0.09) 0.10 0.11 (0.12) 0.13 0.14 (0.15) 0.16 0.17

Harcourt Brace School Publishers

Think About It

The decimal point is missing from each of the numbers in Exercises 1–8.
Place the decimal point where it belongs in each number.

1. **3.5** Number of seconds it takes Tony to write his name

2. **1 7.7** Length of a new pencil in centimeters

3. **1.7 7** Length of a bee in centimeters

4. **2 0.3 6** Record speed in seconds for the 200-meter run

5. **$ 1.2 5** Cost of a fancy helium-filled balloon

6. **3.4 0** Number of miles walked in one hour

7. **3 4.0** Number of miles driven in one hour

8. **1 3 7.1** Height of an average fourth-grade student in centimeters

In Exercises 9–14, arrange
the digits shown to make the
specified number.

1 2 3 4 and 5

9. Smallest number possible

1 2 . 3 4

10. Largest number possible

5 4 . 3 2

11. Number nearest to 30

3 1 . 2 4

12. Greatest number that is less than 35

3 4 . 5 2

13. Smallest number that is greater than 20

2 1 . 3 4

14. Number nearest to 10

1 2 . 3 4

15. What would your answers to Exercises 9–14 be if a card with a zero was
substituted for the 5 card?

01.23; 43.21; 30.12; 34.21; 20.13; 10.23

Harcourt Brace School Publishers

Decimal Drift

Large numbers are often written with both numerals and words. This can make the numbers easier to read.

Example: 34,000,000 may be written as 34 million.

Large numbers can also be written with decimals and words to make them easier to read.

Examples: 34,500,000 = 34.5 million

1,400,000 = 1.4 million

4,800,000 = 4.8 million

The table below shows the areas of the continents in square miles.

1. Complete the table by writing the missing numbers.

Continent	Area (in square miles)	Area (in square miles)
North America	9,400,000	**9.4 million**
South America	6,900,000	**6.9 million**
Europe	**3,800,000**	3.8 million
Asia	**17,400,000**	17.4 million
Africa	11,700,000	**11.7 million**
Oceania, including Australia	3,300,000	3.3 million
Antarctica	5,400,000	**5.4 million**

Use the table to answer Exercises 2–5.

2. Which continent has the greatest area? _____ **Asia** _____

3. Which continent has the least area? _____ **Oceania** _____

4. How many continents have a greater area than North America? __**2**__

5. Which 2 continents together have about the same area as North America?

_____ **Europe and Antarctica** _____

Harcourt Brace School Publishers

First-Second-Third

At the recent Number Olympics, people were confused by who was in first, second, and third place. (Hint: *First* was always the least number and *third* the greatest number.)

Event	Scores	Event	Scores
Number Put	0.3, 0.4, 0.2	Fraction Jump	0.96, 1.53, 0.8
Decimal Hurdles	0.23, 0.45, 0.36	Area Swim	0.6, 0.62, 1.0
High Number	0.3, 0.28, 0.4	Number Beam	3.5, 3.05, 3.47
Freestyle Numbers	1.23, 0.84, 1.1	Perimeter Jog	2.34, 2.4, 2.05

For each event listed, put the numbers in their proper places on the medals stand.

Number Put

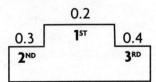

Fraction Jump

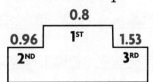

Decimal Hurdles

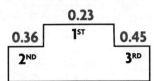

Area Swim

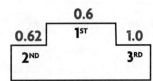

High Number

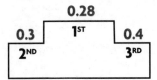

Number Beam

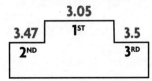

Freestyle Numbers

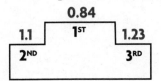

Perimeter Jog

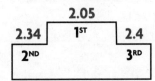

Harcourt Brace School Publishers

Money Combos

Show three different coin combinations that equal each amount below. Use quarters, dimes, nickels, and pennies—at least one of each coin—in each combination.

Answers will vary.

1. $0.84

   <u>2 quarters, 2 dimes, 2 nickels, 4 pennies</u>

   <u>2 quarters, 1 dime, 4 nickels, 4 pennies</u>

   <u>1 quarter, 5 dimes, 1 nickel, 4 pennies</u>

2. $0.55

   <u>1 quarter, 2 dimes, 1 nickel, 5 pennies</u>

   <u>1 quarter, 1 dime, 3 nickels, 5 pennies</u>

   <u>1 quarter, 1 dime, 1 nickel, 15 pennies</u>

3. $1.37

   <u>4 quarters, 3 dimes, 1 nickel, 2 pennies</u>

   <u>4 quarters, 2 dimes, 3 nickels, 2 pennies</u>

   <u>3 quarters, 3 dimes, 6 nickels, 2 pennies</u>

4. $2.46

   <u>9 quarters, 1 dime, 2 nickels, 1 penny</u>

   <u>8 quarters, 3 dimes, 3 nickels, 1 penny</u>

   <u>7 quarters, 5 dimes, 4 nickels, 1 penny</u>

Harcourt Brace School Publishers

Addition and Subtraction Puzzles

Put the numbers in the boxes so that you can either add or
subtract from left to right or top to bottom and get the
same answer below and on the right.

Example:

0.2, 0.3, 0.7, 0.2

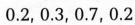

| 0.7 | 0.3 | 0.4 | $0.7 - 0.3 = 0.4$ |
| 0.2 | 0.2 | 0.4 | $0.2 + 0.2 = 0.4$ |

0.5   0.5

$0.3 + 0.2 = 0.5$

$0.7 - 0.2 = 0.5$

1. 1.1, 0.5, 0.2, 0.8

1.1	0.5	0.6
0.8	0.2	0.6
0.3	0.3	

2. 1.7, 0.5, 0.6, 0.6

1.7	0.5	1.2
0.6	0.6	1.2
1.1	1.1	

3. 0.2, 0.2, 1.3, 0.9

1.3	0.9	0.4
0.2	0.2	0.4
1.1	1.1	

4. 0.9, 1.1, 1.3, 0.7

1.3	1.1	0.2
0.9	0.7	0.2
0.4	0.4	

5. 0.9, 0.3, 1.2, 1.8

1.8	1.2	0.6
0.9	0.3	0.6
0.9	0.9	

6. 0.6, 0.6, 1.2, 1.2

1.2	0.6	1.8
0.6	1.2	1.8
1.8	1.8	

7. 0.2, 0.2, 0.3, 0.3

0.3	0.2	0.5
0.2	0.3	0.5
0.5	0.5	

8. 1.3, 1.1, 0.7, 0.5

1.3	0.7	0.6
1.1	0.5	0.6
0.2	0.2	

Harcourt Brace School Publishers

STRETCH YOUR THINKING   **E141**

Amazing Mazes

Fill in the empty boxes by looking at the number patterns.

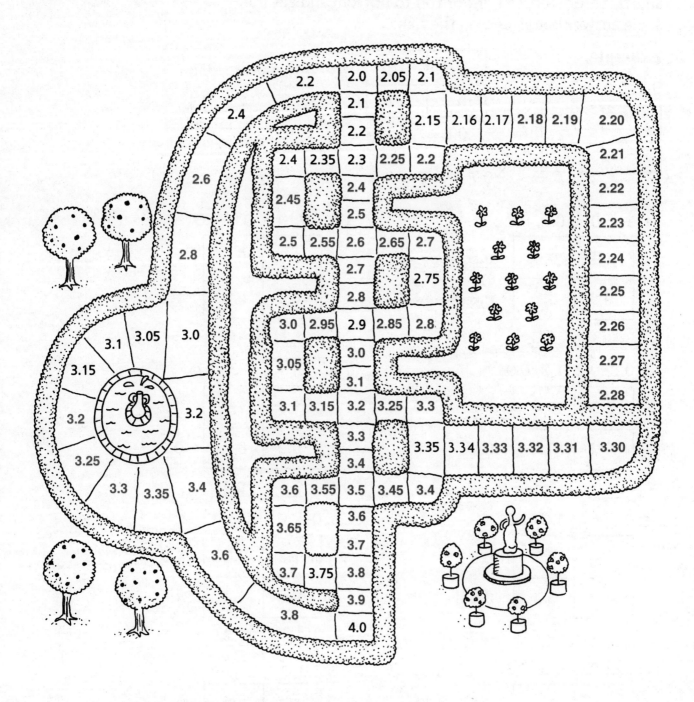

Harcourt Brace School Publishers

Polygon Perimeters

Use the numbers in the box to label the sides of each figure.
The perimeter of each figure is listed. You may want to use a
centimeter ruler.

> 1.2 cm, 1.2 cm, 1.3 cm, 1.3 cm, 1.3 cm, 1.3 cm, 2.3 cm, 2.3 cm,
> 2.3 cm, 2.4 cm, 2.4 cm, 2.4 cm, 2.5 cm, 2.5 cm, 2.5 cm, 2.5 cm,
> 3.1 cm, 3.2 cm, 3.2 cm, 3.8 cm, 5 cm, and 4.7 cm

Square

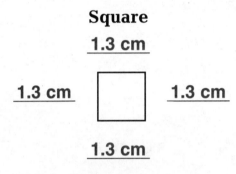

1.3 cm

1.3 cm   1.3 cm

1.3 cm

Perimeter = 5.2 cm

Triangle

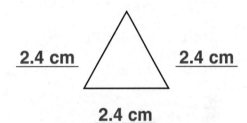

2.4 cm   2.4 cm

2.4 cm

Perimeter = 7.2 cm

Parallelogram

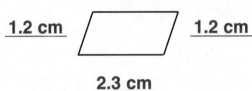

2.3 cm

1.2 cm   1.2 cm

2.3 cm

Perimeter = 7.0 cm

Rectangle

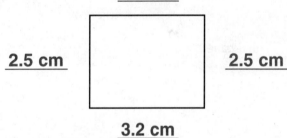

3.2 cm

2.5 cm   2.5 cm

3.2 cm

Perimeter = 11.4 cm

Triangle

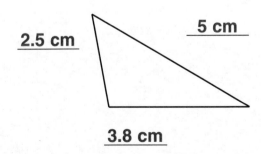

2.5 cm   5 cm

3.8 cm

Perimeter = 11.3 cm

Trapezoid

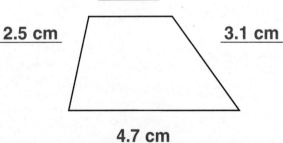

2.3 cm

2.5 cm   3.1 cm

4.7 cm

Perimeter = 12.6 cm

Harcourt Brace School Publishers

Play Ball

0.72   0.9   1.04   1.3   1.16   1.48   2.20

Place the numbers on the balls in the correct spot in the diagram below so that the sum of these positions is the same: **The sum b is always equal to 3.06.**

- All of the outfield = b
- Catcher + Pitcher + Third Base + Left field = b
- Catcher + Pitcher + Shortstop + Center field = b
- Catcher + Pitcher + Second Base + Right field = b
- Catcher + Pitcher + First Base = b

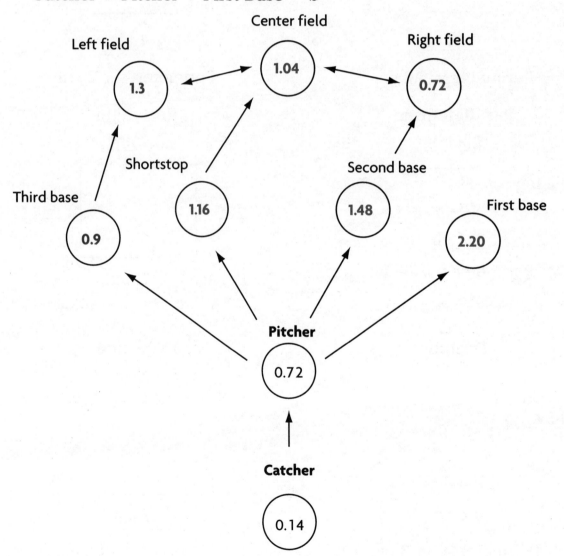

Harcourt Brace School Publishers

Pathy-logical Paths

1. Measure every path to the nearest inch or half inch.
Write the length on the path.

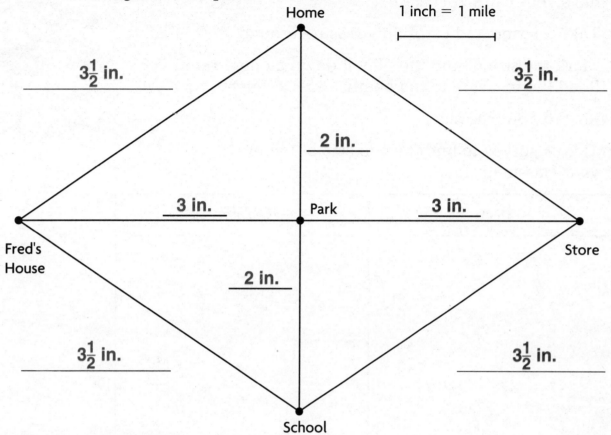

$3\frac{1}{2}$ in.

$3\frac{1}{2}$ in.

1 inch = 1 mile

Home

2 in.

3 in.   Park   3 in.

Fred's
House

Store

2 in.

$3\frac{1}{2}$ in.

$3\frac{1}{2}$ in.

School

2. List four ways to drive from home to school, following these guidelines. Always travel down and to the right or left. Do not retrace your path. **Possible answers:**
   home – Fred's – school; home – Fred's – park – school;
   home – Fred's – park – store – school; home – park – Fred's – school;
   home – park – store – school; home – park – school; home – store – school;
   home – store – park – school; home – store – park – Fred's – school

3. What is the longest route? How many miles is it?
   home – Fred's – park – store – school, or home – store – park –
   Fred's – school; 13 mi

4. What is the shortest route? How long is it?

   home – park – school; 4 mi

5. About how long would it take you to walk the shortest route

   to school? HINT: It takes about 20 minutes to walk a mile. **about 80 min**

Harcourt Brace School Publishers

Cap This!

YOU WILL NEED string 24 inches long, ruler

What's your cap size?

- Take a string and carefully measure around your head.

- Mark the string, and then lay it down along a ruler. Read the measure to the nearest quarter inch.

- Record your cap size.

- Take a survey to find the cap size of ten of your classmates.

Name	Cap Size

What is the average cap size for the ten classmates in your survey? Explain. You may use a calculator.

Answers will vary.

_____

_____

_____

_____

_____

Harcourt Brace School Publishers

Ring-A-Ling

When you graph your phone number, does it make a geometric pattern?

YOU WILL NEED grid paper

On a piece of grid paper, follow these directions.

• Start in the center of the grid paper.

• Use the digits in your phone number to decide how far to move in each direction. Write your phone number four times in a row.

• Move up (↑), then right (→), then down (↓), then left (←). Continue this process until there are no more digits.

For example:

The phone number 321-4123 would make the following moves:

• 3 up, 2 right, 1 down, 4 left, 1 up, 2 right, 3 down

• The result is the figure at the right.

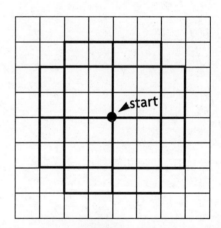

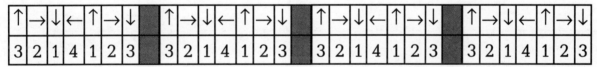

Write your phone number 4 times. Graph your numbers. Compare your completed geometric pattern with the one shown above and with one of your classmates'. **Check students' graphs.**

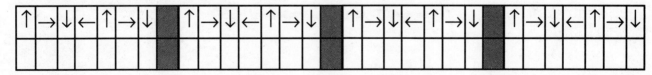

Harcourt Brace School Publishers

Biking Adventure

1. Sammy is going on a week-long bicycle trip with his dad.
They plan to ride from Acton to Halpine by going
through Brattle, Capeville, Dawson, Easton, Foxboro, and
Grafton. Then they will go straight back to Acton from
Halpine. They made a detailed map of the route. Use the
information below to find out how far they will ride.

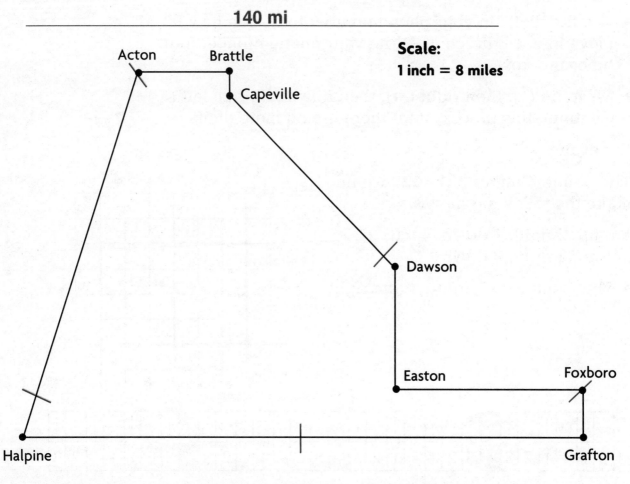

140 mi

Scale:
1 inch = 8 miles

2. If Sammy and his dad bicycle the same distance each day
for five days, how many miles will they travel in one day?

28 mi

3. Make dash marks on the map to show about how far
Sammy and his dad rode each day. **Check students'
drawings.**

Harcourt Brace School Publishers

Half Full or Half Empty?

The pitchers below are the same size. They are arranged from barely full to completely full. Each pitcher can be labeled with two equal measurements. Use the measures in the box to write in the missing measurement for each pitcher.

18 cups, 8 quarts, 12 quarts,
2 gallons, 3 gallons, 3 quarts, 16 cups

1.

3 pints or 6 cups

2.

6 pints or **3 quarts**

3.

1 gallon or **16 cups**

4.

9 pints or **18 cups**

5.

2 gallons or **8 quarts**

6.

3 gallons or **12 quarts**

Which Weight?

The weights belong on the balance scales. Some of the scales are unbalanced. Match one weight listed below with one exercise to make a true statement.

16 ounces, 32 ounces, 48 ounces, 52 ounces, 96 ounces, 5 pounds, 4,000 pounds, 8 tons

1.

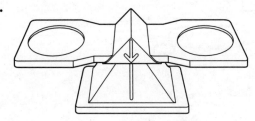

2 pounds = __32 ounces__

2.

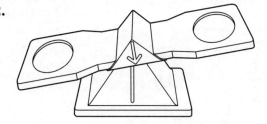

24 ounces > __16 ounces__

3.

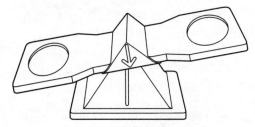

4 pounds > __52 ounces__

4.

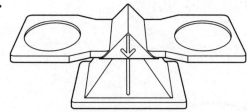

2 tons = __4,000 pounds__

5.

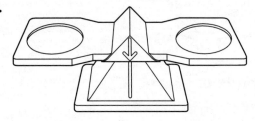

6 pounds = __96 ounces__

6.

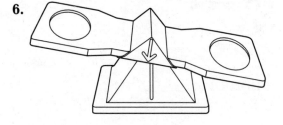

6 tons < __8 tons__

7.

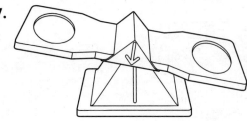

24 ounces < __5 pounds__

8.

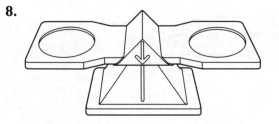

3 pounds = __48 ounces__

Harcourt Brace School Publishers

Point A to Point B

1. Measure and record the lengths of each line to the nearest centimeter and decimeter.

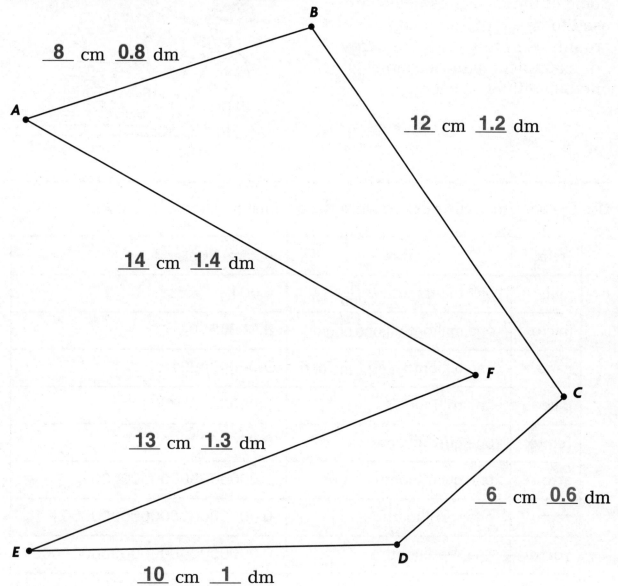

__8__ cm __0.8__ dm

__12__ cm __1.2__ dm

__14__ cm __1.4__ dm

__13__ cm __1.3__ dm

__6__ cm __0.6__ dm

__10__ cm __1__ dm

2. Start at *A* and measure clockwise until you are back at *A*.

a. How many centimeters is this measure? __63 cm__

b. How many decimeters is this measure? __6.3 dm__

c. How many times would you need to measure around

this figure to read a measure of 5 meters? __8 times__

Harcourt Brace School Publishers

STRETCH YOUR THINKING E151

Below Centi–

Milli means "one thousandth". $0.001 = \frac{1}{1000}$

Some of the measures below are used to measure microscopic organisms or tiny units of energy. For example, a nanosecond is one billionth of a second.

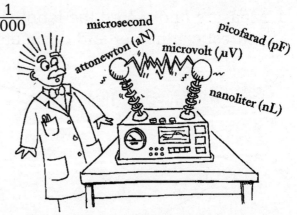

Use the pattern in the table to write the decimal numbers.

1.

Prefix	Unit	Decimal Number
milli	one thousandth $\frac{1}{1,000}$	0.001
micro	one millionth $\frac{1}{1,000,000}$	**0.000001**
nano	one billionth $\frac{1}{1,000,000,000}$	**0.000000001**
pico	one trillionth	**0.000000000001**
femto	one quadrillionth	**0.000000000000001**
atto	one quintillionth	0.000000000000000001
zepto	one sextillionth	0.000000000000000000001
yocto	one septillionth	0.000000000000000000000001

2. How many micrometers equal 1 millimeter ? ___**1,000**___

3. Look at the table. Write the next two decimal numbers to follow one septillionth. Just for fun, make up a prefix to name your two numbers.

Prefixes will vary. 0.000000000000000000000000001;
_____

0.0000000000000000000000000000001

Harcourt Brace School Publishers

Wedding Fun

Sam and Sarah are getting married. Their friends are tying cans to the back of their car. How many meters long is the rope they are using?

_____ 3 m _____

To find out:

- Place the numbers in order from least to greatest in the cake.

- Fill in the squares from left to right and from bottom to top.

- Add the numbers in the starred boxes to find how long the rope is.

7 dm, 250 cm, 1 m, 5 cm, 0.6 m,
1 dm, 180 cm, 14 dm, 0.28 m,
20 dm, 88 cm, 32 cm, 3 dm,
120 cm, 15 cm, 210 cm, 2 cm,
9.0 dm, 0.01 m, 2.15 m, 4.8 dm

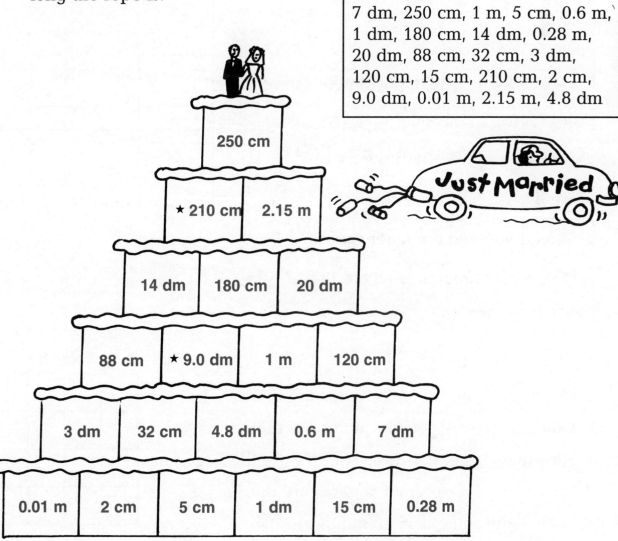

250 cm		
★ 210 cm	2.15 m	
14 dm	180 cm	20 dm

88 cm	★ 9.0 dm	1 m	120 cm

3 dm	32 cm	4.8 dm	0.6 m	7 dm

0.01 m	2 cm	5 cm	1 dm	15 cm	0.28 m

Harcourt Brace School Publishers

Squares Galore

For Figures A–C, find all possible squares.

1. Look at Figure *A*.

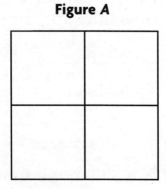

Figure A

   a. How many one-by-one squares are there? __4__

   b. How many two-by-two squares are there? __1__

   c. How many squares in all are there? __5__

2. Look at Figure *B*.

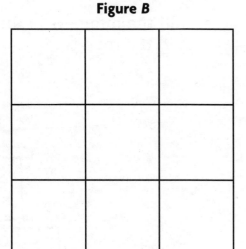

Figure B

   a. How many one-by-one squares
   are there? __9__

   b. How many two-by-two squares
   are there? __4__

   c. How many three-by-three squares
   are there? __1__

   d. Should you add the outer square? __no__

   e. How many squares in all are there? __14__

3. Look at Figure *C*.

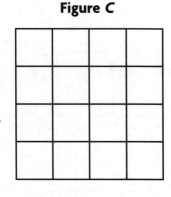

Figure C

   a. How many one-by-one squares are there? __16__

   b. How many two-by-two squares are there? __9__

   c. How many three-by-three squares are there? __4__

   d. How many four-by-four squares are there? __1__

   e. How many squares in all are there? __30__

Harcourt Brace School Publishers

Punch All Around

Fruity-Tutty Punch Recipe

1 liter orange juice
1 metric cup pineapple juice
2 metric cups apple juice
100 milliliters kiwi juice
50 milliliters lemon juice
2 liters seltzer water

1. List the recipe ingredients from least to greatest.

   lemon juice, kiwi juice, pineapple juice, apple juice,

   orange juice, seltzer water

2. How much punch will the recipe make, in milliliters?
   in liters? _____ **3,900 mL; 3.9 L**

3. A punch glass holds about 300 mL. About how many

   glasses does the recipe serve? _____ **about 13 glasses**

4. You sell a glass of punch for $0.50. How much
   money will you take in if you sell an entire recipe

   of punch? _____ **$6.50**

5. It costs $4.87 for all the punch ingredients. How much

   money will you make? _____ **$1.63**

6. Your punch is so popular, you are asked to make
   enough for 100 glasses. How many times will you

   need to increase the recipe? _____ **8 times**

7. You charge $0.75 a glass. How much money will

   you take in? _____ **$75.00**

8. Your cost for all the ingredients is $38.96. How

   much money will you make? _____ **$36.04**

Harcourt Brace School Publishers

Name _____

Sweet Enough

How many sugar packs would it take to balance each object?

1 g

1.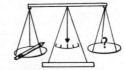

1 gram = __**1 sugar pack**__

2.

2.3 kg = __**2,300 sugar packs**__

3.

80 kg = __**80,000 sugar packs**__

4.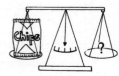

25 g = __**25 sugar packs**__

Write the mass in *g* and *kg*.

5. 100 sugar packs = __**100 g and**__
__**0.1 kg**__

6. 300 sugar packs = __**300 g and**__
__**0.300 kg**__

7. 250 sugar packs = __**250 g and**__
__**0.25 kg**__

8. 1,000 sugar packs = __**1,000 g and**__
__**1 kg**__

9. 3,000 sugar packs = __**3,000 g**__
__**and 3 kg**__

10. 5,000 sugar packs = __**5,000 g**__
__**and 5 kg**__

Find the number of sugar packs in each box.

11.

__**25,000 sugar packs**__

12.

__**16,000 sugar packs**__

13.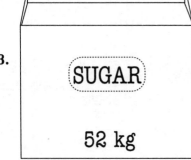

__**52,000 sugar packs**__

Harcourt Brace School Publishers

E156   STRETCH YOUR THINKING

Time Zones

The earth is divided into 24 longitudinal time zones. When it's noon in your hometown, it's midnight on the other side of the earth. Here's a sampling of times from other time zones when it is 12:00 noon in London.

Honolulu
2:00 A.M.

Los Angeles
3:00 A.M.

Denver
4:00 A.M.

Chicago
5:00 A.M.

New York
6:00 A.M.

London
Noon

Tokyo
9:00 P.M.

Auckland
Midnight

Answer the following questions based on the clocks above.

1. If it is 8:00 A.M. in London, what time is it in

   a. Denver? __12:00 A.M.__

   b. Honolulu? __10:00 P.M.__

   c. Tokyo? __5:00 P.M.__

2. If it is 12:00 noon in New York, what time is it in

   a. Auckland? __6:00 A.M.__

   b. Los Angeles? __9:00 A.M.__

   c. Tokyo? __3:00 A.M.__

3. If it is 6:00 P.M. in Honolulu, what time is it in

   a. London? __4:00 A.M.__

   b. Chicago? __9:00 P.M.__

   c. Denver? __8:00 P.M.__

4. If it is 5:00 P.M. in Auckland, what time is it in

   a. Los Angeles? __8:00 P.M.__

   b. New York? __11:00 P.M.__

   c. London? __5:00 A.M.__

Harcourt Brace School Publishers

Who Won the Race?

In short races like the 100-meter dash, racers often finish within a fraction of a second of each other. Times are established by lane, and then sorted from first to last.

Sort the following finishes, labeling the times 1 (first place) through 8 (last place).

Race 1	Time	Place		Race 2	Time	Place
Lane 1	10.01	7		Lane 1	9.98	6 – tie
Lane 2	9.89	2		Lane 2	9.83	1
Lane 3	9.94	5		Lane 3	9.93	5
Lane 4	9.86	1		Lane 4	9.87	2
Lane 5	9.93	4		Lane 5	9.89	3
Lane 6	9.95	6		Lane 6	9.92	4
Lane 7	10.14	8		Lane 7	10.02	8
Lane 8	9.91	3		Lane 8	9.98	6 – tie

Now look at the times for both races, and list the top 7 times.

Place	Race	Lane	Time
1	2	2	9.83
2	1	4	9.86
3	2	4	9.87
4	2	5	9.89
5	1	2	9.89
6	1	8	9.91
7	2	6	9.92

(4 and 5 marked "tie")

Harcourt Brace School Publishers

Measuring the Solar System

Since the orbit of the planets in our solar system around the Sun is not a circle, the distance from planet to Sun constantly changes. Here are the average distances of planets to the Sun.

Sun to Mercury	36,000,000 miles
Sun to Venus	67,000,000 miles
Sun to Earth	93,000,000 miles
Sun to Mars	141,000,000 miles
Sun to Jupiter	483,300,000 miles
Sun to Saturn	886,400,000 miles
Sun to Uranus	1,786,000,000 miles
Sun to Neptune	2,794,000,000 miles
Sun to Pluto	3,660,000,000 miles

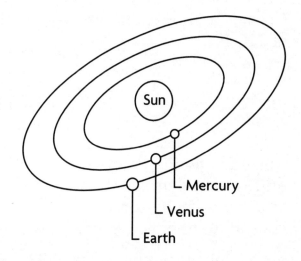

1. Which two planets' orbits are closest together? how close?

   Earth and Venus; 26,000,000 mi

2. Which two planets that are next to each other have the greatest distance between their orbits? how far?

   Uranus and Neptune; 1,008,000,000 mi

3. How many miles are between the orbits of

   a. Earth and Mars?   **48,000,000 mi**

   b. Mercury and Venus?   **31,000,000 mi**

   c. Jupiter and Saturn?   **403,100,000 mi**

4. Is the Earth closer to Mars or Mercury?

   Mars

5. If you could travel at the rate of 1 million miles per day, about how many days would it take to get to Uranus?

   about 1,693 days

Harcourt Brace School Publishers

Heating Up

Temperature is measured in degrees Fahrenheit (°F) in the United States. Water freezes at 32°F and boils at 212°F.

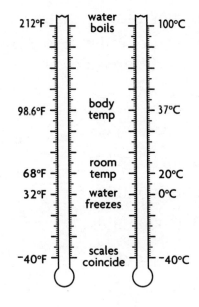

212°F — water boils — 100°C

98.6°F — body temp — 37°C

68°F — room temp — 20°C
32°F — water freezes — 0°C

−40°F — scales coincide — −40°C

Temperature is measured in degrees Celsius (°C) in countries that use the metric system and by scientists. Water freezes at 0°C and boils at 100°C.

You can change temperatures from degrees °C to degrees °F by using a special number sentence.

1.8 × Celsius temperature + 32 = ⬚ °F

To change 25°C to degrees °F, substitute and solve.

(1.8 × 25) + 32 ⟶ 45 + 32 = 77   So, 25°C = 77°F.

Write which temperature best describes the activity.

1. ice hockey, 30°C or 30°F

_____30°F_____

2. running, 50°C or 50°F

_____50°F_____

3. surfing, 40°C or 40°F

_____40°C_____

4. swimming, 30°C or 30°F

_____30°C_____

Rewrite °C to °F and answer the question. Use a calculator.

5. Your pen pal in Japan writes that it is 20°C outside. What is the temperature in °F? Does she need to wear a jacket?

___1.8 × 20 + 32 = 68°F; probably doesn't need a jacket___

6. You write to your pen pal in Nebraska where it is 9°C. What is the temperature in °F? Does your pen pal need a jacket?

___48.2°F; probably needs a jacket___

Harcourt Brace School Publishers

Puzzlement

You can solve geometric puzzles using toothpicks
or pencils.

Puzzle 1: Create five identical squares by removing only four sticks.

Puzzle 2: Create three identical squares by moving—not removing—
four sticks. Two solutions exist. Can you find them both?

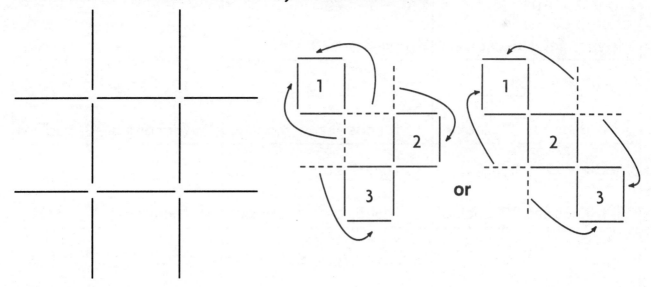

Harcourt Brace School Publishers

Cookie Giveaway

You have 210 cookies to give equally to friends. There can be no cookies left over. How many different groups can you make?

Write your groupings in the table. You may use a calculator.

	Groupings Table	
210 ÷ 2 = 105 2 friends get 105 cookies	210 ÷ 3 = 70 3 friends get 70 cookies	210 ÷ 5 = 42 5 friends get 42 cookies
210 ÷ 6 = 35 6 friends get 35 cookies	210 ÷ 7 = 30 7 friends get 30 cookies	210 ÷ 10 = 21 10 friends get 21 cookies
210 ÷ 14 = 15 14 friends get 15 cookies	210 ÷ 15 = 14 15 friends get 14 cookies	210 ÷ 21 = 10 21 friends get 10 cookies
210 ÷ 30 = 7 30 friends get 7 cookies	210 ÷ 35 = 6 35 friends get 6 cookies	210 ÷ 42 = 5 42 friends get 5 cookies
210 ÷ 70 = 3 70 friends get 3 cookies	210 ÷ 105 = 2 105 friends get 2 cookies	210 ÷ 210 = 1 210 friends get 1 cookie

Harcourt Brace School Publishers

Division Patterns

Find the quotient. Look for a pattern.

1. $4\overline{)4}$ **1 r0**

2. $4\overline{)5}$ **1 r1**

3. $4\overline{)6}$ **1 r2**

4. $4\overline{)7}$ **1 r3**

5. $4\overline{)8}$ **2 r0**

6. $4\overline{)9}$ **2 r1**

7. $4\overline{)10}$ **2 r2**

8. $4\overline{)11}$ **2 r3**

9. $4\overline{)12}$ **3 r0**

10. $4\overline{)13}$ **3 r1**

11. $4\overline{)14}$ **3 r2**

12. $4\overline{)15}$ **3 r3**

Use the pattern in the answers for Exercises 1–12 to help you
write the answers to Exercises 13–20.

13. $4\overline{)16}$ **4 r0**

14. $4\overline{)17}$ **4 r1**

15. $4\overline{)18}$ **4 r2**

16. $4\overline{)19}$ **4 r3**

17. $4\overline{)20}$ **5 r0**

18. $4\overline{)21}$ **5 r1**

19. $4\overline{)22}$ **5 r2**

20. $4\overline{)23}$ **5 r3**

Solve.

21. $4\overline{)40}$ **10 r0**

$4\overline{)41}$ **10 r1**

$4\overline{)42}$ **10 r2**

$4\overline{)43}$ **10 r3**

$4\overline{)45}$ **11 r1**

22. $40\overline{)50}$ **1 r10**

$40\overline{)60}$ **1 r20**

$40\overline{)70}$ **1 r30**

$40\overline{)80}$ **2 r0**

$40\overline{)90}$ **2 r10**

23. $4\overline{)51}$ **12 r3**

$4\overline{)15}$ **3 r3**

$5\overline{)41}$ **8 r1**

$5\overline{)14}$ **2 r4**

$2\overline{)51}$ **25 r1**

24. Look at the answers for the five division problems in

Exercise 21. Is there a pattern? __yes__

25. Look at the answers for the five division problems in

Exercise 22. Is there a pattern? __yes__

26. Look at the answers for the five division problems in

Exercise 23. Is there a pattern? __no__

Harcourt Brace School Publishers

Puzzled

Trace and cut out each of the figures below. See if you can build
an 8-by-8 square. Record your final square on the grid below.

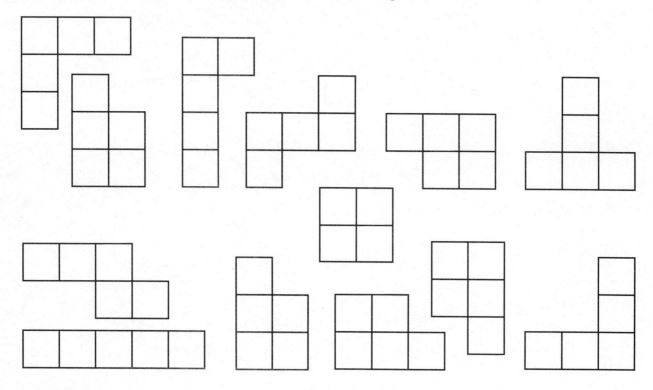

Possible solution:

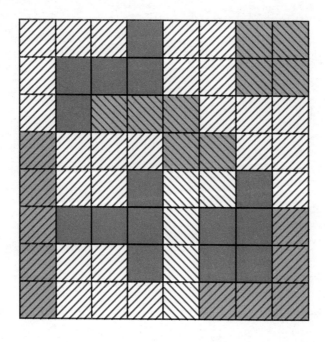

Harcourt Brace School Publishers

Evenly Divided

How many ways can you divide a square
into four equal pieces? Try to find at
least six different ways. **Solutions may
vary. Possible solutions are shown.**

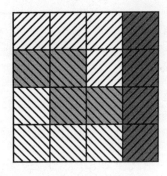

1.

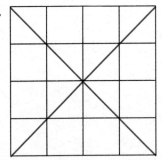

2.

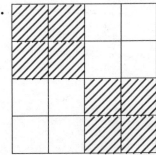

3.

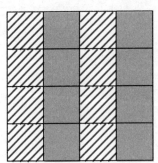

4.

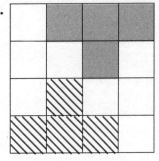

5.

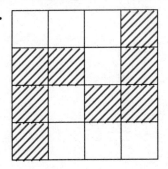

6.

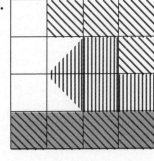

Harcourt Brace School Publishers

Time Flies

60 seconds = 1 minute	365 days = 1 year
60 minutes = 1 hour	52 weeks = 1 year
24 hours = 1 day	12 months = 1 year
30 days = 1 month	

How many seconds old is each item below?

Write a number sentence and solve. You may use a calculator. **Number sentences may vary.**

1.

10 years old today

$10 \times 365 \times 24 \times 60 \times 60 =$

315,360,000; 315,360,000 sec

2.

3 years old

$3 \times 365 \times 24 \times 60 \times 60 =$

94,608,000; 94,608,000 sec

3.

2 hours old

$2 \times 60 \times 60 =$

7,200; 7,200 sec

4.

85 years old

$85 \times 365 \times 24 \times 60 \times 60 =$

2,680,560,000; 2,680,560,000 sec

5.

3 days old

$3 \times 24 \times 60 \times 60 =$

259,200; 259,200 sec

6.

2 weeks old

$7 \times 2 \times 24 \times 60 \times 60 =$

1,209,600; 1,209,600 sec

Harcourt Brace School Publishers

Division Cipher

Each shape in the exercises below represents a number 0–9.
Use your multiplication and division skills to find what number
each shape represents. Then fill in the key.

Key

1.

trapezoid = 0, pentagon = 1, diamond = 2, triangle = 3, hexagon = 4,

___ ___ ___ ___ ___

2.

parallelogram = 5, square = 6, star = 7, octagon = 8, circle = 9

___ ___ ___ ___ ___

Solve.

3.

```
        ⟨2⟩  △3
    ×   ⟨1⟩  △3
    ─────────────
        [6]  (9)
    + ⟨2⟩ △3 ⟨0⟩ (trap)
    ─────────────
      ⟨2⟩ (9) (9)
```

4.

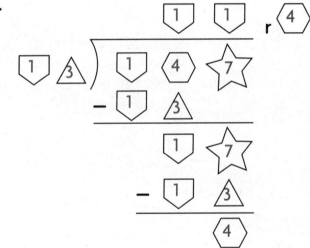

5.

```
          △3  ⟨4⟩
      ×   ⟨2⟩  /5/
    ─────────────────
      ⟨1⟩  ☆7  /0/(trap)
    + [6] (8) /0/(trap)
    ─────────────────
      (8) /5/ /0/(trap)
```

6.

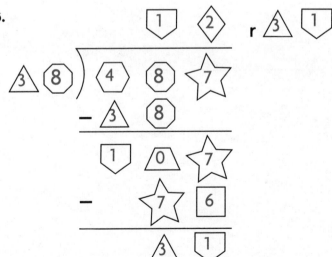

Harcourt Brace School Publishers

Fraction Free-for-All

Play this game with a partner. You will
need fraction-circle pieces, a pencil, and
a paper clip. Follow the game rules below.

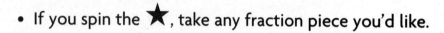

Game Rules

- Take turns.

- Use the paper clip and your pencil on
  the spinner to spin for a fraction.

- Find the fraction piece equal to the
  fraction spun. Place that fraction piece
  on one of the two circles below if it will fit.

- If you spin the ★, take any fraction piece you'd like.

- The first player to cover both circles with fraction pieces wins.

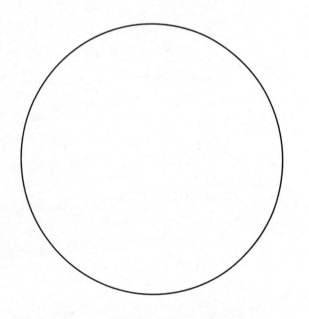
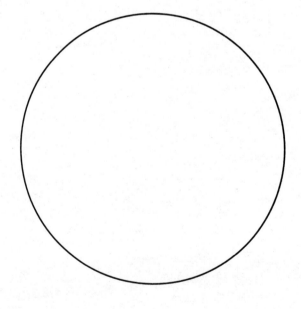

Harcourt Brace School Publishers

Survey Fun

The graph shows that sports is the favorite camp activity for $\frac{4}{6}$ of the 12 fourth graders. How many fourth graders like sports best?

Find $\frac{4}{6}$ of 12. $\frac{4}{6}$ ←numerator
                          ←denominator

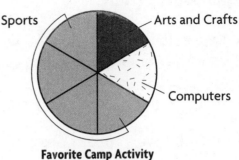

**Favorite Camp Activity
of 12 Fourth Graders**

- Look at the denominator. Divide 12 into that number of equal groups. Find how many in each group.

$12 \div 6 = 2$ 2 in each group

- Look at the numerator. Multiply 4 by the number in each group. Find how many are in that number of groups.

$4 \times 2 = 8$ 8 in 4 groups

So, $\frac{4}{6}$ of 12 is 8. Of the fourth graders, 8 like sports best.

Use the circle graphs to answer.

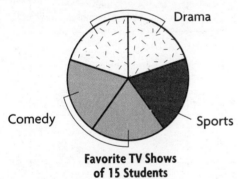

**Favorite TV Shows
of 15 Students**

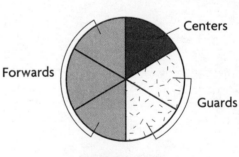

**12 Players of the
Waltham Basketball Team**

1. students who like comedy best

   fraction ___$\frac{2}{5}$___

   number of students __6__

2. students who like sports best

   fraction ___$\frac{1}{5}$___

   number of students __3__

3. number of forwards

   fraction ___$\frac{3}{6}$, or $\frac{1}{2}$___

   number of players __6__

4. number of guards

   fraction ___$\frac{2}{6}$, or $\frac{1}{3}$___

   number of players __4__

Harcourt Brace School Publishers

Decimals in Disguise

You can use a calculator to help you write a fraction as a decimal. Simply divide the numerator by the denominator.

Here are some examples:

$\frac{3}{8} \rightarrow$ | 3 | ÷ | 8 | = | 0.375 | So, $\frac{3}{8} = 0.375$.

$\frac{2}{5} \rightarrow$ | 2 | ÷ | 5 | = | 0.4 | So, $\frac{2}{5} = 0.4$.

You may use a calculator. Write each fraction in the first grid as a decimal in the second grid.

1.

$\frac{3}{8}$	$\frac{2}{4}$	$\frac{6}{8}$
$\frac{1}{2}$	$\frac{3}{5}$	$\frac{1}{8}$
$\frac{1}{5}$	$\frac{5}{8}$	$\frac{3}{4}$

0.375	0.5	0.75
0.5	0.6	0.125
0.2	0.625	0.75

2.

$\frac{2}{5}$	$\frac{4}{8}$	$\frac{3}{6}$
$\frac{7}{8}$	$\frac{2}{2}$	$\frac{4}{5}$
$\frac{1}{4}$	$\frac{3}{10}$	$\frac{2}{8}$

0.4	0.5	0.5
0.875	1.0	0.8
0.25	0.3	0.25

3. For which two fractions did you write the decimal 0.75? _____ $\frac{6}{8}$ and $\frac{3}{4}$ _____

4. Write another fraction that can also be written as the decimal 0.75.

any fraction equivalent to $\frac{3}{4}$, such as $\frac{9}{12}$, $\frac{12}{16}$, or $\frac{15}{20}$

5. In each decimal grid in Exercises 1 and 2, draw a straight line through the three decimals whose sum is 1.55. **See the grids in Exercises 1 and 2.**

Harcourt Brace School Publishers

Musical Survey

Todd asked 10 people which instruments they like to listen to the most—piano, guitar, or saxophone. Here is what the people answered:

Piano	Guitar	Saxophone
IIII	III	III

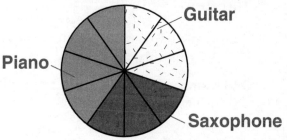

Becky — guitar   Jonah — guitar

Damari — piano   Kenny — saxophone

Jacki — piano   Ho — saxophone

Kerry — saxophone Tanisha — guitar

Scott — piano   Brooke — piano

Instruments 10 People

Like to Listen to the Most

1. Use the table above to tally the number of votes for each instrument. Then complete the graph to show the data. **Check students' tallies and graphs.**

2. Write a sentence describing what the data in the graph show.
Possible answer: An equal number of people like listening to guitar and to saxophone.

3. Write a question to ask ten people. Give them three or four choices for answers.

Check students' questions.

4. Survey ten people. Record the data in the table. Make a graph to show the data. **Check students' tables and graphs.**

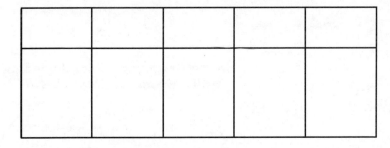
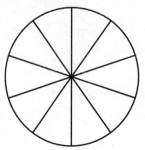

5. Write a sentence describing what the data in your survey graph show.

Sentences will vary, but should describe the graph in Exercise 4.

Harcourt Brace School Publishers

Venn Diagrams

Venn diagrams show how groups of items are related.

- An attribute is associated with each circle of the diagram, and items with that attribute are placed in the circle.

- Items that have more than one of the attributes are placed in an area where the circles overlap.

Odd Numbers Between   **Multiples of 5**
     0 and 20   **Between 0 and 28**

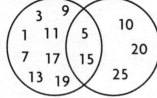

For Exercises 1–2, use the Venn diagram below.

1. List the numbers in each group.

   Factors of 12: _____ **1, 2, 3, 4, 6, 12** _____

   Multiples of 3 less than 20: _____ **3, 6, 9, 12, 15, 18** _____

2. Write the numbers from Exercise 1 in the Venn diagram.

                  Multiples of 3
Factors of 12   **Less Than 20**

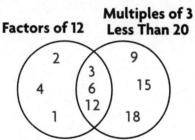

For Exercises 3–4, use the *Months* Venn diagram.

3. List the months in each group.
   Names of months beginning with a vowel:

   _____ **Apr, Aug, Oct** _____

   Names of months ending with the letter *r*:

   _____ **Sep, Oct, Nov, Dec** _____

4. Write the months in the Venn diagram.

Months Beginning   **Months Ending**
 with a Vowel   **with Letter *R***

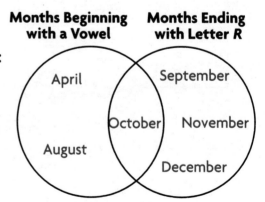

Harcourt Brace School Publishers